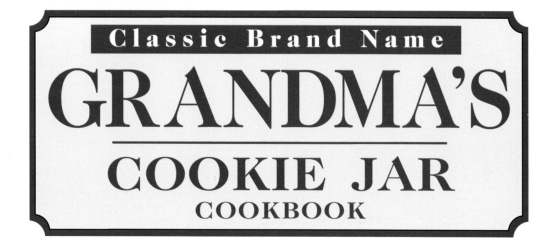

# Classic Brand Name

# GRANDMA'S

## COOKIE JAR
### COOKBOOK

Publications International, Ltd.

**Microwave Cooking:** Microwave ovens vary in wattage. Use the cooking times as guidelines and check for doneness before adding more time.

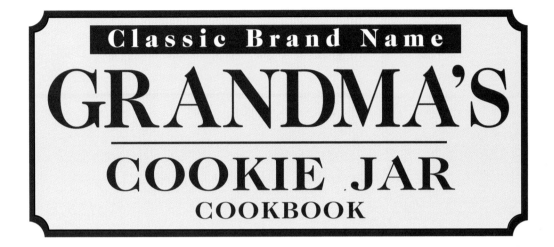

**Classic Brand Name**

# GRANDMA'S
## COOKIE JAR
### COOKBOOK

# All-Time Favorites

❧❦❧

## Almond–Orange Shortbread

**1 cup (4 ounces) sliced almonds, divided**
**2 cups all-purpose flour**
**1 cup cold butter, cut into pieces**
**½ cup sugar**
**½ cup cornstarch**
**2 tablespoons grated orange peel**
**1 teaspoon almond extract**

**1.** Preheat oven to 350°F. Spread ¾ cup almonds in single layer in large baking pan. Bake 6 minutes or until golden brown, stirring frequently. Cool completely in pan. *Reduce oven temperature to 325°F.*

**2.** Place toasted almonds in food processor. Process using on/off pulsing action until almonds are coarsely chopped.

**3.** Add flour, butter, sugar, cornstarch, orange peel and almond extract to food processor. Process using on/off pulsing action until mixture resembles coarse crumbs.

**4.** Press dough firmly and evenly into 10×8½-inch rectangle on large ungreased cookie sheet with fingers. Score dough into 1¼-inch squares with knife. Press one slice of remaining almonds in center of each square.

**5.** Bake 30 to 40 minutes or until shortbread is firm when pressed and lightly browned. Immediately cut into squares along score lines with sharp knife. Remove cookies to wire racks; cool completely.

**6.** Store loosely covered at room temperature up to 1 week.

*Makes about 5 dozen cookies*

*Almond-Orange Shortbread*

## FUDGY RAISIN PIXIES

½ cup butter, softened
2 cups granulated sugar
4 eggs
2 cups all-purpose flour, divided
¾ cup unsweetened cocoa powder
2 teaspoons baking powder
½ teaspoon salt
½ cup chocolate-covered raisins
   Powdered sugar

Beat butter and granulated sugar in large bowl until light and fluffy. Add eggs; mix until well blended. Combine 1 cup flour, cocoa, baking powder and salt in small bowl; add to butter mixture. Mix until well blended. Stir in remaining 1 cup flour and chocolate-covered raisins. Cover; refrigerate until firm, 2 hours or overnight.

Preheat oven to 350°F. Grease cookie sheets. Coat hands with powdered sugar. Shape rounded teaspoonfuls of dough into 1-inch balls; roll in powdered sugar. Place 2 inches apart on prepared cookie sheets. Bake 14 to 17 minutes or until firm to the touch. Remove immediately from cookie sheets; cool completely on wire racks.

*Makes about 4 dozen cookies*

## OATMEAL SCOTCHIES

1 cup (2 sticks) margarine or butter, softened
¾ cup granulated sugar
¾ cup firmly packed brown sugar
2 eggs
1 teaspoon vanilla *or* 2 teaspoons grated orange peel (about 1 orange)
1¼ cups all-purpose flour
1 teaspoon baking soda
½ teaspoon salt (optional)
½ teaspoon ground cinnamon
3 cups QUAKER® Oats (quick or old fashioned, uncooked)
1 (12-ounce) package (2 cups) NESTLE® TOLL HOUSE® Butterscotch Flavored Morsels

Heat oven to 375°F. Beat together margarine, sugars, eggs and vanilla until creamy. Gradually add combined flour, baking soda, salt and cinnamon; mix well. Stir in remaining ingredients. Drop by level measuring tablespoonfuls onto ungreased cookie sheet. Bake 7 to 8 minutes for a chewy cookie or 9 to 10 minutes for a crisp cookie. Cool 2 minutes on cookie sheet; remove to wire rack. Cool completely.

*Makes about 4 dozen cookies*

## CHOCOLATE CHIP COOKIES

8 tablespoons margarine, softened
1½ cups packed light brown sugar
2 egg whites
1 teaspoon vanilla
2½ cups all-purpose flour
1½ teaspoons baking soda
½ teaspoon salt
⅓ cup fat-free (skim) milk
¾ cup (4 ounces) semisweet chocolate chips
½ cup chopped pecans or walnuts (optional)

**1.** Preheat oven to 350°F. Spray cookie sheets with nonstick cooking spray.

**2.** Beat margarine and brown sugar in large bowl until fluffy. Beat in egg whites and vanilla.

**3.** Combine flour, baking soda and salt in medium bowl. Add flour mixture to margarine mixture alternately with milk, ending with flour mixture. Stir in chocolate chips and pecans.

**4.** Drop dough by slightly rounded tablespoonfuls onto prepared cookie sheets. Bake about 10 minutes or until lightly browned. Cool on wire racks.

*Makes about 6 dozen cookies*

*Chocolate Chip Cookies*

## HOLIDAY SUGAR COOKIES

1 cup butter, softened
¾ cup sugar
1 egg
2 cups all-purpose flour
1 teaspoon baking powder
¼ teaspoon ground cinnamon
¼ teaspoon salt
  Colored sprinkles or sugar, for
    decorating (optional)

Beat butter and sugar in large bowl with electric mixer until creamy. Add egg; beat until fluffy.

Stir in flour, baking powder, cinnamon and salt until well blended. Form dough into a ball; wrap in plastic wrap and flatten. Refrigerate about 2 hours or until firm.

Preheat oven to 350°F. Roll out dough, a small portion at a time, to ¼-inch thickness on lightly floured surface with lightly floured rolling pin. (Keep remaining dough wrapped in refrigerator.)

Cut out cookies with 3-inch cookie cutter. Sprinkle with colored sprinkles or sugar, if desired. Transfer to ungreased cookie sheets.

Bake 7 to 9 minutes until edges are lightly browned. Let cookies stand on cookie sheets 1 minute; transfer to wire racks to cool completely. Store in airtight container.

*Makes about 3 dozen cookies*

## CHEWY OATMEAL RAISIN COOKIES

1 cup packed light brown sugar
1 cup FLEISCHMANN'S® Original
    Margarine, softened
¼ cup EGG BEATERS® Healthy Real
    Egg Substitute
1 teaspoon vanilla extract
2 cups quick-cooking oats
1½ cups all-purpose flour
1 teaspoon baking soda
1 teaspoon ground cinnamon
1 cup seedless raisins

1. Beat sugar and margarine in large bowl with mixer at medium speed until blended. Beat in egg substitute and vanilla until mixture is smooth.

2. Blend in oats, flour, baking soda and cinnamon. Stir in raisins.

3. Drop batter by tablespoonfuls, 2 inches apart, onto greased baking sheets. Bake in preheated 400°F oven for 5 to 7 minutes or until lightly browned. Remove from sheets; cool on wire racks.

*Makes about 3 dozen cookies*

**Preparation Time:** 25 minutes
**Cook Time:** 20 minutes

## BUTTERY ALMOND CUTOUTS

1 cup butter, softened
1½ cups granulated sugar
¾ cup sour cream
2 eggs
3 teaspoons almond extract, divided
1 teaspoon vanilla
4⅓ cups all-purpose flour
1 teaspoon baking powder
1 teaspoon baking soda
½ teaspoon salt
2 cups powdered sugar
2 tablespoons milk
1 tablespoon light corn syrup
Food color

**1.** Beat butter and granulated sugar in large bowl until light and fluffy. Add sour cream, eggs, 2 teaspoons almond extract and vanilla; beat until smooth. Add combined flour, baking powder, baking soda and salt; beat just until well blended.

**2.** Divide dough into 4 pieces; flatten each piece into disc. Wrap with plastic wrap. Refrigerate at least 3 hours.

**3.** Combine powdered sugar, milk, corn syrup and remaining 1 teaspoon almond extract in small bowl. Cover and refrigerate.

**4.** Preheat oven to 375°F. Working with 1 disc at a time, roll dough out onto floured surface to ¼-inch thickness. Cut into desired shapes using 2½-inch cookie cutters. Place about 2 inches apart onto ungreased cookie sheets. Bake 7 to 8 minutes or until edges are firm and bottoms are brown. Remove from cookie sheets to wire rack to cool.

**5.** Separate powdered sugar mixture into 3 or 4 batches in small bowls; tint each batch with desired food color. Frost cookies.

*Makes about 3 dozen cookies*

## PEANUT BUTTER CHOCOLATE CHIP COOKIES

¼ cup butter or margarine, softened
¼ cup shortening
½ cup REESE'S® Creamy Peanut Butter
½ cup packed light brown sugar
½ cup granulated sugar
1 egg
1¼ cups all-purpose flour
¾ teaspoon baking soda
½ teaspoon baking powder
2 cups (12-ounce package) HERSHEY'S® Semi-Sweet Chocolate Chips
Granulated sugar

Heat oven to 375°F.

In large mixer bowl beat butter, shortening, peanut butter, brown sugar, ½ cup granulated sugar and egg until light and fluffy. Stir together flour, baking soda and baking powder; add to butter mixture. Stir in chocolate chips (if necessary, with hands work chocolate chips into batter).

Shape into 1-inch balls; place on ungreased cookie sheet. With fork dipped in granulated sugar flatten slightly in criss-cross pattern.

Bake 9 to 11 minutes or just until set. Cool slightly; remove from cookie sheet to wire rack. Cool completely.

*Makes about 3 dozen cookies*

## OATMEAL TOFFEE LIZZIES

¾ Butter Flavor* CRISCO® Stick or ¾ cup
   Butter Flavor* CRISCO® all-vegetable
   shortening plus additional for
   greasing
1¼ cups firmly packed light brown sugar
 1 egg
⅓ cup milk
1½ teaspoons vanilla
 3 cups quick oats, uncooked
 1 cup all-purpose flour
½ teaspoon baking soda
½ teaspoon salt
1½ cups semi-sweet chocolate chips
½ cup almond brickle chips
½ cup finely chopped pecans

*Butter Flavor Crisco® is artificially flavored.*

**1.** Heat oven to 375°F. Grease baking sheets
with shortening. Place sheets of foil on
countertop for cooling cookies.

**2.** Combine ¾ cup shortening, brown sugar,
egg, milk and vanilla in large bowl. Beat at
medium speed of electric mixer until well
blended.

**3.** Combine oats, flour, baking soda and salt.
Mix into creamed mixture at low speed just
until blended. Stir in chocolate chips, almond
chips and pecans.

**4.** Shape dough into 1¼- to 1½-inch balls with
lightly floured hands. Place 2 inches apart
onto prepared baking sheet. Flatten slightly.

**5.** Bake one baking sheet at a time at 375°F for
10 to 12 minutes, or until lightly browned. *Do
not overbake.* Cool 2 minutes on baking sheet.
Remove cookies to foil to cool completely.
*Makes about 2½ dozen cookies*

## BUTTERY ALMOND COOKIES

1¼ cups all-purpose flour
½ teaspoon baking powder
⅛ teaspoon salt
10 tablespoons butter, softened
¾ cup sugar
 1 egg
 1 teaspoon vanilla
¾ cup slivered almonds, finely chopped
½ cup slivered almonds, for garnish

Preheat oven to 350°F. Grease cookie sheets.
Combine flour, baking powder and salt in
small bowl.

Beat butter in large bowl with electric mixer
at medium speed until smooth. Gradually
beat in sugar until blended; increase speed to
high and beat until light and fluffy. Beat in
egg until fluffy. Beat in vanilla until blended.
Stir in flour mixture until blended. Stir in
chopped almonds just until combined.

Drop rounded teaspoonfuls of dough about
2 inches apart onto prepared cookie sheets.
Top each cookie with several slivered almonds,
pressing into dough.

Bake 12 minutes or until edges are golden
brown. Let cookies stand on cookie sheets
5 minutes; transfer to wire racks to cool
completely. Store in airtight container.
*Makes about 3½ dozen cookies*

## HERSHEY'S MILK CHOCOLATE CHIP GIANT COOKIES

    6 tablespoons butter, softened
½ cup granulated sugar
¼ cup packed light brown sugar
½ teaspoon vanilla extract
 1 egg
 1 cup all-purpose flour
½ teaspoon baking soda
 2 cups (11.5-ounce package) HERSHEY'S
    Milk Chocolate Chips
    Frosting (optional)
    Ice cream (optional)

**1.** Heat oven to 350°F. Line two 9-inch round baking pans with foil, extending foil over edge of pans.

**2.** Beat butter, granulated sugar, brown sugar and vanilla until light and fluffy. Add egg; beat well. Stir together flour and baking soda; gradually add to butter mixture, beating until well blended. Stir in milk chocolate chips. Spread one half of batter into each prepared pan, spreading to 1 inch from edge. (Cookies will spread to edge when baking.)

**3.** Bake 15 to 20 minutes or until lightly browned. Cool completely; carefully lift cookies from pan and remove foil. Frost, if desired. Cut each cookie into wedges; serve topped with scoop of ice cream, if desired.

*Makes about 12 to 16 servings*

**Tip:** Bake cookies on the middle rack of oven, one pan at a time. Uneven browning can occur if baking on more than one rack at the same time.

## PECAN COOKIES

1¼ cups confectioners' sugar
 1 Butter Flavor* CRISCO® Stick or 1 cup
    Butter Flavor CRISCO® all-vegetable
    shortening
 2 eggs
¼ cup light corn syrup or regular pancake
    syrup
 1 tablespoon vanilla
 2 cups all-purpose flour
1½ cups finely chopped pecans
¾ teaspoon baking powder
½ teaspoon baking soda
½ teaspoon salt
    Confectioners' sugar

*Butter Flavor Crisco® is artificially flavored.*

**1.** Heat oven to 350°F. Place sheets of foil on countertop for cooling cookies.

**2.** Place confectioners' sugar and 1 cup shortening in large bowl. Beat at medium speed of electric mixer until well blended. Add eggs, syrup and vanilla; beat until well blended and fluffy.

**3.** Combine flour, pecans, baking powder, baking soda and salt. Add to shortening mixture; beat at low speed until well blended.

**4.** Shape dough into 1-inch balls. Place 2 inches apart on ungreased baking sheet.

**5.** Bake for 15 to 18 minutes or until bottoms of cookies are light golden brown. *Do not overbake.* Cool 2 minutes on baking sheet. Roll in confectioners' sugar while warm. Remove cookies to foil to cool completely. Reroll in confectioners' sugar prior to serving.

*Makes about 4 dozen cookies*

*Hershey's Milk Chocolate Chip Giant Cookie*

## BUTTERSCOTCH COOKIES WITH BURNT BUTTER ICING

½ cup butter, softened
1½ cups packed brown sugar
2 eggs
1 teaspoon vanilla
2½ cups flour
1 teaspoon baking soda
½ teaspoon salt
1 cup dairy sour cream
1 cup finely chopped walnuts
Burnt Butter Icing (recipe follows)

Beat butter and brown sugar until light and fluffy. Blend in eggs and vanilla; mix well. Add combined dry ingredients alternately with sour cream, mixing well after each addition. Stir in nuts. Chill 4 hours or overnight. Drop rounded teaspoonfuls of dough, 3 inches apart, onto well buttered cookie sheet. Bake at 400°F for 8 to 10 minutes or until lightly browned. Cool. Frost with Burnt Butter Icing.          *Makes 5 dozen cookies*

**Burnt Butter Icing:** Melt 6 tablespoons butter in small saucepan over medium heat; continue heating until golden brown. Cool. Blend in 2 cups sifted powdered sugar, 2 tablespoons hot water and 1 teaspoon vanilla. Add enough additional hot water, a little at a time, until spreading consistency is reached.

*Favorite recipe from* **Wisconsin Milk Marketing Board**

## PEANUT BUTTER OATMEAL TREATS

1¾ cups all-purpose flour
1 teaspoon baking soda
½ teaspoon salt
½ cup butter or margarine, softened
½ cup SMUCKER'S® Creamy Natural Peanut Butter or LAURA SCUDDER'S® Smooth Old-Fashioned Peanut Butter
1 cup sugar
1 cup firmly packed light brown sugar
2 eggs
¼ cup milk
1 teaspoon vanilla
2½ cups uncooked oats
1 cup semi-sweet chocolate chips

Combine flour, baking soda and salt; set aside. In large mixing bowl, combine butter, peanut butter, sugar and brown sugar. Beat until light and creamy. Beat in eggs, milk and vanilla. Stir in flour mixture, oats and chocolate chips. Drop dough by rounded teaspoonfuls about 3 inches apart onto ungreased cookie sheets. Bake at 350°F for 15 minutes or until lightly browned.          *Makes 3½ dozen cookies*

## COCOA SNICKERDOODLES

1 cup butter, softened
¾ cup packed brown sugar
¾ cup plus 2 tablespoons granulated
    sugar, divided
2 eggs
2 cups uncooked rolled oats
1½ cups all-purpose flour
¼ cup plus 2 tablespoons unsweetened
    cocoa powder, divided
1 teaspoon baking soda
2 tablespoons ground cinnamon

Preheat oven to 375°F. Lightly grease cookie sheets or line with parchment paper.

Beat butter, brown sugar and ¾ cup granulated sugar in large bowl until light and fluffy. Add eggs; mix well. Combine oats, flour, ¼ cup cocoa and baking soda in medium bowl. Stir into butter mixture until blended.

Mix remaining 2 tablespoons granulated sugar, remaining 2 tablespoons cocoa and cinnamon in small bowl. Drop dough by rounded teaspoonfuls into cinnamon mixture; toss to coat. Place 2 inches apart on prepared cookie sheets.

Bake 8 to 10 minutes or until firm in center. *Do not overbake.* Remove to wire racks to cool.

*Makes about 4½ dozen cookies*

## WHITE CHOCOLATE CHIP & MACADAMIA COOKIES

2 squares (1 ounce each) unsweetened
    chocolate
½ cup butter, softened
1 cup packed light brown sugar
1 egg
1 teaspoon vanilla
1¼ cups all-purpose flour
½ teaspoon baking soda
1 cup (6 ounces) white chocolate chips
¾ cup macadamia nuts, chopped

Preheat oven to 350°F. Lightly grease cookie sheets or line with parchment paper. Melt unsweetened chocolate in top of double boiler over hot, not boiling, water. Remove from heat; cool. Cream butter, melted chocolate and sugar in large bowl until blended. Add egg and vanilla; beat until light. Blend in flour, baking soda, chocolate chips and macadamia nuts. Drop dough by rounded teaspoonfuls 2 inches apart onto prepared cookie sheets. Bake 10 to 12 minutes or until firm. *Do not overbake.* Remove to wire racks to cool. *Makes about 4 dozen cookies*

## LEMONY BUTTER COOKIES

½ cup butter, softened
½ cup sugar
1 egg
1½ cups all-purpose flour
1 teaspoon grated lemon peel
2 tablespoons fresh lemon juice
½ teaspoon baking powder
⅛ teaspoon salt
   Additional sugar

Beat butter and sugar in large bowl with electric mixer until creamy. Beat in egg until light and fluffy. Mix in flour, lemon peel and juice, baking powder and salt. Cover; refrigerate about 2 hours or until firm.

Preheat oven to 350°F. Roll out dough, a small portion at a time, on well-floured surface to ¼-inch thickness. (Keep remaining dough in refrigerator.) Cut with 3-inch round cookie cutter. Transfer to ungreased cookie sheets. Sprinkle with sugar.

Bake 8 to 10 minutes or until lightly browned on edges. Cool 1 minute on cookie sheets. Remove to wire racks; cool completely. Store in airtight container.

*Makes about 2½ dozen cookies*

## CHOCOLATE CHIPS COOKIES WITH MACADAMIA NUTS

⅔ cup butter or margarine, softened
½ cup packed light brown sugar
½ cup granulated sugar
1 teaspoon vanilla extract
1 egg
1 cup all-purpose flour
⅓ cup HERSHEY'S Cocoa
½ teaspoon baking soda
½ teaspoon salt
2 cups (12-ounce package) HERSHEY'S Semi-Sweet Chocolate Chips
¾ cup (3½-ounce jar) macadamia nuts, coarsely chopped

1. Beat butter, brown sugar, granulated sugar and vanilla in large bowl until creamy. Add egg; blend well.

2. Stir together flour, cocoa, baking soda and salt; gradually add to butter mixture, blending well. Stir in chocolate chips and nuts. Cover; refrigerate 1 to 2 hours.

3. Heat oven to 350°F. Very lightly grease cookie sheet. Using ice cream scoop or ¼ cup measuring cup, drop dough onto prepared cookie sheet; flatten slightly.

4. Bake 10 to 12 minutes. (Do not overbake; cookies will be soft. They will puff during baking and flatten upon cooling.) Cool slightly; remove from cookie sheet to wire rack. Cool completely.

*Makes about 1 dozen cookies*

*Lemony Butter Cookies*

## SWEDISH SANDWICH COOKIES (SYLTKAKOR)

1 cup butter, softened
½ cup plus 2 tablespoons sugar, divided
1 large egg yolk
1 large egg, separated
2 to 2¼ cups all-purpose flour
3 tablespoons ground almonds
3 tablespoons red currant or strawberry jelly

**1.** Grease and flour cookie sheets; set aside. Beat butter and ½ cup sugar in large bowl with electric mixer at medium speed until light and fluffy. Beat in egg yolks.

**2.** Gradually add 1½ cups flour; beat at low speed until well blended. Stir in additional flour with spoon to form stiff dough. Form dough into 2 discs; wrap in plastic wrap and refrigerate until firm, at least 2 hours.

**3.** Preheat oven to 375°F. Unwrap 1 disc and place on lightly floured surface. Roll out dough with lightly floured rolling pin to ⅛-inch thickness.

**4.** Cut dough with floured 2¼-inch *round* cookie cutter. Place cookies 1½ to 2 inches apart on prepared cookie sheets. Gently knead dough trimmings together; reroll and cut out more cookies.

**5.** Repeat step 3 with second disc.

**6.** Cut dough with floured 2¼-inch *scalloped* cookie cutter. Cut 1-inch centers out of scalloped cookies. Place cookies 1½ to 2 inches apart on prepared cookie sheets. (Cut equal numbers of round and scalloped cookies.)

**7.** Beat egg white in small cup with wire whisk. Combine almonds and remaining 2 tablespoons sugar in small bowl. Brush each scalloped cookie with egg white; sprinkle with sugar mixture. Bake cookies 8 to 10 minutes or until firm and light golden brown. Remove cookies to wire racks; cool completely.

**8.** To assemble cookies, spread about ½ teaspoon currant jelly over flat side of round cookies; top with flat side of scalloped cookies to form sandwich.

**9.** Store tightly covered at room temperature or freeze up to 3 months.

*Makes 1½ dozen sandwich cookies*

*To reduce the risk of overprocessing when grinding nuts in a food processor or blender, add a small amount of the flour or sugar from the recipe.*

*Swedish Sandwich Cookies (Syltkakor)*

# CHOCOLATE SENSATIONS

### CHOCOLATE CRACKLETOPS

2 cups all-purpose flour
2 teaspoons baking powder
2 cups granulated sugar
½ cup (1 stick) butter or margarine
4 squares (1 ounce each) unsweetened baking chocolate, chopped
4 large eggs, lightly beaten
2 teaspoons vanilla extract
1¾ cups "M&M's"® Chocolate Mini Baking Bits
Additional granulated sugar

Combine flour and baking powder; set aside. In 2-quart saucepan over medium heat combine 2 cups sugar, butter and chocolate, stirring until butter and chocolate are melted; remove from heat. Gradually stir in eggs and vanilla. Stir in flour mixture until well blended. Chill mixture 1 hour. Stir in "M&M's"® Chocolate Mini Baking Bits; chill mixture an additional 1 hour.

Preheat oven to 350°F. Line cookie sheets with foil. With sugar-dusted hands, roll dough into 1-inch balls; roll balls in additional granulated sugar. Place about 2 inches apart onto prepared cookie sheets. Bake 10 to 12 minutes. *Do not overbake.* Cool completely on wire racks. Store in tightly covered container.                    *Makes about 5 dozen cookies*

*Chocolate Crackletops*

## RASPBERRY–FILLED CHOCOLATE RAVIOLI

1 cup butter, softened
½ cup granulated sugar
2 squares (1 ounce each) bittersweet or semisweet chocolate, melted and cooled
1 egg
1 teaspoon vanilla
½ teaspoon chocolate extract
¼ teaspoon baking soda
   Dash salt
2½ cups all-purpose flour
1 to 1¼ cups seedless raspberry jam
   Powdered sugar

Mix butter and granulated sugar in large bowl until blended. Add melted chocolate, egg, vanilla, chocolate extract, baking soda and salt; beat until light. Blend in flour to make stiff dough. Divide dough in half. Cover; refrigerate until firm.

Preheat oven to 350°F. Lightly grease cookie sheets or line with parchment paper. Roll out dough, half at a time, ⅛ inch thick between two sheets of plastic wrap. Remove top sheet of plastic. (If dough gets too soft and sticks to plastic, refrigerate until firm.) Cut dough into 1½-inch squares. Place half of the squares, 2 inches apart, on prepared cookie sheets. Place about ½ teaspoon jam on center of each square; top with another square. Using fork, press edges of squares together to seal, then pierce center of each square. Bake 10 minutes or just until edges are browned. Remove to wire racks to cool. Dust lightly with powdered sugar.

*Makes about 6 dozen ravioli*

## WHITE CHOCOLATE BIGGIES

1½ cups butter, softened
1 cup granulated sugar
¾ cup packed light brown sugar
2 eggs
2 teaspoons vanilla
2½ cups all-purpose flour
⅔ cup unsweetened cocoa powder
1 teaspoon baking soda
½ teaspoon salt
1 package (10 ounces) large white chocolate chips *or* 1 white chocolate bar, cut into pieces
¾ cup pecan halves, coarsely chopped
½ cup golden raisins

Preheat oven to 350°F. Lightly grease cookie sheets or line with parchment paper.

Beat butter, sugars, eggs and vanilla in large bowl until light and fluffy. Combine flour, cocoa, baking soda and salt in medium bowl; blend into butter mixture until smooth. Stir in white chocolate chips, pecans and raisins.

Scoop out about ⅓ cup dough for each cookie. Place on prepared cookie sheets, spacing about 4 inches apart. Press each cookie to flatten slightly.

Bake 12 to 14 minutes or until firm in center. Cool 5 minutes on cookie sheets; remove to wire racks to cool completely.

*Makes about 2 dozen cookies*

*Raspberry-Filled Chocolate Ravioli*

## CHOCOLATE THUMBPRINT COOKIES

½ cup (1 stick) butter or margarine,
  softened
⅔ cup sugar
1 egg, separated
2 tablespoons milk
1 teaspoon vanilla extract
1 cup all-purpose flour
⅓ cup HERSHEY'S Cocoa
¼ teaspoon salt
1 cup chopped nuts
  Vanilla Filling (recipe follows)
26 HERSHEY'S KISSES Milk Chocolates,
  HERSHEY'S HUGS Chocolates or
  pecan halves or candied cherry halves

**1.** Beat butter, sugar, egg yolk, milk and
vanilla in medium bowl until light and fluffy.
Stir together flour, cocoa and salt; gradually
add to butter mixture, beating until blended.
Refrigerate dough at least 1 hour or until firm
enough to handle.

**2.** Heat oven to 350°F. Lightly grease cookie
sheet. Shape dough into 1-inch balls. With
fork, beat egg white slightly. Dip each ball
into egg white; roll in nuts. Place on prepared
cookie sheet. Press thumb gently in center of
each cookie.

**3.** Bake cookies 10 to 12 minutes or until set.
Meanwhile, prepare Vanilla Filling. Remove
wrappers from chocolate pieces. Remove
cookies from cookie sheet to wire rack; cool
5 minutes. Spoon about ¼ teaspoon prepared
filling into each thumbprint. Gently press
chocolate piece onto top of each cookie. Cool
completely.          *Makes about 2 dozen cookies*

## VANILLA FILLING

½ cup powdered sugar
1 tablespoon butter or margarine,
  softened
2 teaspoons milk
¼ teaspoon vanilla extract

Combine powdered sugar, butter, milk and
vanilla; beat until smooth.

## CHOCOLATE PLATTER COOKIES

1 cup unsalted butter, softened
1 cup packed light brown sugar
½ cup granulated sugar
2 eggs
2⅓ cups all-purpose flour
1 teaspoon baking soda
½ teaspoon salt
1 package (12 ounces) semisweet chocolate
  chunks
2 cups chopped pecans

Preheat oven to 375°F. Lightly grease cookie
sheets or line with parchment paper. Cream
butter with sugars until smooth. Add eggs;
beat until fluffy. Combine flour, baking soda
and salt in small bowl. Add to creamed
mixture, mixing until dough is stiff. Stir in
chocolate chunks and pecans. Scoop out
about ⅓ cupful of dough for each cookie.
Place on prepared cookie sheets, spacing 4
inches apart. Using back of fork, flatten each
cookie to about ½ inch thick. Bake 15 minutes
or until light golden. Remove to wire racks to
cool.          *Makes about 16 cookies*

## COFFEE CHIP DROPS

1¼ cups firmly packed light brown sugar
¾ Butter Flavor* CRISCO® Stick or ¾ cup
    Butter Flavor* CRISCO® all-vegetable
    shortening
2 tablespoons cold coffee
1 teaspoon vanilla
1 egg
1¾ cups all-purpose flour
1 tablespoon finely ground French roast or
    espresso coffee beans
1 teaspoon salt
¾ teaspoon baking soda
½ cup semisweet chocolate chips
½ cup milk chocolate chips
½ cup coarsely chopped walnuts
30 to 40 chocolate kiss candies, unwrapped

*Butter Flavor Crisco® is artificially flavored.*

1. Heat oven to 375°F. Place sheets of foil on countertop for cooling cookies.

2. Place brown sugar, ¾ cup shortening, coffee and vanilla in large bowl. Beat at medium speed of electric mixer until well blended. Add egg; beat well.

3. Combine flour, ground coffee, salt and baking soda. Add to shortening mixture; beat at low speed just until blended. Stir in chocolate chips and walnuts.

4. Drop dough by rounded tablespoonfuls 2 inches apart onto ungreased baking sheets.

5. Bake one baking sheet at a time at 375°F for 8 to 10 minutes or until cookies are lightly browned and just set. *Do not overbake.* Place 1 candy in center of each cookie. Cool 2 minutes on baking sheet. Remove cookies to foil to cool completely.

*Makes about 3 dozen cookies*

## CHOCOLATE CHERRY COOKIES

½ cup butter, softened
½ cup sugar
1 egg
2 squares (1 ounce each) unsweetened
    chocolate, melted and cooled
2 cups cake flour
1 teaspoon vanilla
¼ teaspoon salt
    Maraschino cherries, well drained
    (about 48)
1 cup (6 ounces) semisweet or milk
    chocolate chips

Beat butter and sugar in large bowl until light. Add egg and melted chocolate; beat until fluffy. Stir in cake flour, vanilla and salt until well blended. Cover; refrigerate until firm, about 1 hour.

Preheat oven to 400°F. Lightly grease cookie sheets or line with parchment paper. Shape dough into 1-inch balls. Place 2 inches apart on prepared cookie sheets. With knuckle of finger, make deep indentation in center of each ball. Place cherry into each indentation. Bake 8 minutes or just until set. Meanwhile, melt chocolate chips in small bowl over hot water. Stir until melted. Remove cookies to wire racks. Drizzle melted chocolate over tops of cookies while still warm. Refrigerate until chocolate is set.

*Makes about 4 dozen cookies*

## DOUBLE CHOCOLATE CHUNK COOKIES

2 squares (1 ounce each) unsweetened chocolate
3 eggs
1 cup vegetable oil
¾ cup packed brown sugar
1 teaspoon baking powder
1 teaspoon vanilla
¼ teaspoon baking soda
¼ teaspoon salt
2⅓ cups all-purpose flour
1 package (12 ounces) semisweet chocolate chunks

Preheat oven to 350°F. Lightly grease cookie sheets or line with parchment paper. Melt unsweetened chocolate in top of double boiler over hot, not boiling, water. Remove from heat; cool. Beat eggs in large bowl until foamy. Add oil and sugar; continue beating until light and frothy. Blend in baking powder, vanilla, baking soda, salt and melted chocolate. Mix in flour until smooth. Stir in chocolate chunks. Shape dough into walnut-sized balls. Place 2 inches apart on prepared cookie sheets. Bake 10 to 12 minutes or until firm in center. *Do not overbake.* Remove to wire racks to cool.

*Makes about 4½ dozen cookies*

**White Chocolate Chunk Cookies:** Substitute one package (12 ounces) white chocolate chunks or two white chocolate candy bars (5 to 6 ounces each), cut into chunks, for the semisweet chocolate chunks.

## ALMOND CHOCOLATE KISS COOKIES

½ cup sugar
½ cup margarine or butter, softened
¼ cup egg substitute
1 teaspoon almond extract
1⅓ cups all-purpose flour
1 teaspoon baking soda
½ cup PLANTERS® Slivered Almonds, toasted and finely chopped
24 chocolate candy kisses

**1.** Beat sugar and margarine in large bowl with mixer at medium speed until creamy. Blend in egg substitute and almond extract.

**2.** Mix flour and baking soda in small bowl; stir into egg mixture.

**3.** Shape dough into 1-inch balls; roll in toasted almonds. Place 2 inches apart on ungreased baking sheets. Bake in preheated 350°F oven for 7 to 9 minutes or until lightly golden; remove from oven. Immediately top each cookie with a candy kiss, pressing lightly into center of cookie.

**4.** Remove from sheets. Cool completely on wire racks. Store in airtight container.

*Makes 2 dozen cookies*

**Preparation Time:** 25 minutes
**Cook Time:** 7 minutes
**Total Time:** 32 minutes

*White Chocolate Chunk Cookies*

THE YALE
SHAKESPEARE

KING HENRY
THE FIFTH

EDITED BY
ROBERT D. FRENCH

YALE UNIVERSITY
PRESS

## FUDGEY GERMAN CHOCOLATE SANDWICH COOKIES

1¾ cups all-purpose flour
1½ cups sugar
¾ cup (1½ sticks) butter or margarine, softened
⅔ cup HERSHEY'S Cocoa or HERSHEY'S Dutch Processed Cocoa
¾ teaspoon baking soda
¼ teaspoon salt
2 eggs
2 tablespoons milk
1 teaspoon vanilla extract
½ cup finely chopped pecans
   Coconut and Pecan Filling (recipe follows)

Heat oven to 350°F. In large bowl, combine flour, sugar, butter, cocoa, baking soda and salt, eggs, milk and vanilla. Beat at medium speed of electric mixer until blended (batter will be stiff). Stir in pecans.

Form batter into 1¼-inch balls. Place on ungreased cookie sheet; flatten slightly.

Bake 9 to 11 minutes or until almost set. Cool slightly; remove from cookie sheet to wire rack. Cool completely. Spread about 1 heaping tablespoon Coconut and Pecan Filling onto bottom of one cookie. Top with second cookie to make sandwich. Serve warm or at room temperature.

*Makes about 17 sandwich cookies*

**Prep Time:** 25 minutes
**Bake Time:** 9 minutes
**Cool Time:** 35 minutes

## COCONUT AND PECAN FILLING

½ cup (1 stick) butter or margarine
½ cup packed light brown sugar
¼ cup light corn syrup
1 cup MOUNDS® Sweetened Coconut Flakes, toasted*
1 cup finely chopped pecans
1 teaspoon vanilla extract

*\*To toast coconut: Heat oven to 350°F. Spread coconut in even layer on baking sheet. Bake 6 to 8 minutes, stirring occasionally, until golden.*

In medium saucepan, melt butter; add brown sugar and corn syrup. Stir constantly, until thick and bubbly. Remove from heat; stir in coconut, pecans and vanilla. Use warm.

*Makes about 2 cups filling*

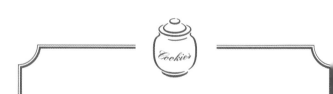

*Grease cookie sheets only if directed to do so in the recipe. Some cookie doughs are high enough in fat that they will not stick to the sheet.*

*Fudgey German Chocolate Sandwich Cookies*

# SIMPLY ELEGANT

❧❀❧

## VIENNESE MERINGUE BARS

1 cup butter, softened
1¼ cups sugar, divided
2 egg yolks
¼ teaspoon salt
2¼ cups all-purpose flour
1 cup seedless raspberry jam
1½ cups mini semisweet chocolate chips
3 egg whites
½ cup slivered almonds, toasted

Preheat oven to 350°F. Beat butter and ½ cup sugar in large bowl with electric mixer at medium speed until light and fluffy. Beat in egg yolks and salt. Gradually add flour. Beat at low speed until well blended.

With buttered fingers, pat dough evenly into ungreased 15×10-inch jelly-roll pan. Bake 22 to 25 minutes or until light golden brown. Remove from oven; immediately spread jam over crust. Sprinkle evenly with chocolate chips.

For meringue topping, beat egg whites in clean large bowl with electric mixer on high speed until foamy. Gradually beat in remaining ¾ cup sugar until stiff peaks form. Gently stir in almonds with rubber spatula.

Spoon meringue over chocolate mixture; spread evenly with small spatula. Bake 20 to 25 minutes or until golden brown. Cool completely on wire rack. Cut into bars. *Makes 28 bars*

*Viennese Meringue Bar*

## CHOCOLATE ALMOND BISCOTTI

**3 cups all-purpose flour**
**½ cup unsweetened cocoa**
**2 teaspoons baking powder**
**½ teaspoon salt**
**1 cup granulated sugar**
**⅔ cup FLEISCHMANN'S® Original**
    **Margarine, softened**
**¾ cup EGG BEATERS® Healthy Real Egg**
    **Substitute**
**1 teaspoon almond extract**
**½ cup whole blanched almonds, toasted**
    **and coarsely chopped**
    **Powdered Sugar Glaze (recipe follows)**

In medium bowl, combine flour, cocoa, baking powder and salt; set aside.

In large bowl, with electric mixer at medium speed, beat granulated sugar and margarine for 2 minutes or until creamy. Add Egg Beaters® and almond extract; beat well. With electric mixer at low speed, gradually add flour mixture, beating just until blended; stir in almonds.

On lightly greased baking sheet, form dough into two (12×2½-inch) logs. Bake at 350°F for 25 to 30 minutes or until toothpick inserted in centers comes out clean. Remove from sheet; cool on wire racks 15 minutes.

Using serrated knife, slice each log diagonally into 12 (1-inch-thick) slices; place, cut sides up, on same baking sheet. Bake at 350°F for 12 to 15 minutes on each side or until cookies are crisp and edges are browned. Remove from sheet; cool completely on wire rack. Drizzle tops with Powdered Sugar Glaze.

*Makes 2 dozen cookies*

**Powdered Sugar Glaze:** In small bowl, combine 1 cup powdered sugar and 5 to 6 teaspoons water until smooth.

**Prep Time:** 25 minutes
**Cook Time:** 45 minutes

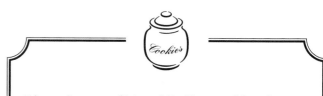

*Biscotti are traditional Italian cookies that are baked twice to produce their characteristic crunchy texture. They are ideal for dipping in coffee, tea or dessert wine.*

*Chocolate Almond Biscotti*

## ESPRESSO CHOCOLATE CHIP KISSES

1¼ cups firmly packed light brown sugar
¾ Butter Flavor* CRISCO® Stick or ¾ cup
    Butter Flavor* CRISCO® all-vegetable
    shortening
2 tablespoons milk
1 teaspoon vanilla
½ teaspoon brandy extract
1 egg
1¾ cups all-purpose flour
1 teaspoon instant coffee
1 teaspoon salt
¾ teaspoon baking soda
⅓ cup milk chocolate chips
⅓ cup semi-sweet chocolate chips
½ cup coarsely chopped walnuts
    (optional)**
32 chocolate kisses, unwrapped

*Butter Flavor Crisco® is artificially flavored.*

**If nuts are omitted, add an additional ½ cup semi-sweet chocolate chips.*

**1.** Heat oven to 375°F. Place sheets of foil on countertop for cooling cookies.

**2.** Combine brown sugar, ¾ cup shortening, milk, vanilla and brandy extract in large bowl. Beat at medium speed of electric mixer until well blended. Beat egg into creamed mixture.

**3.** Combine flour, instant coffee, salt and baking soda. Mix into creamed mixture just until blended. Stir in milk chocolate chips, semi-sweet chocolate chips and walnuts.

**4.** Drop rounded measuring tablespoonfuls of dough 3 inches apart onto ungreased baking sheets.

**5.** Bake one baking sheet at a time at 375°F for 8 to 10 minutes for chewy cookies, or 11 to 13 minutes for crisp cookies. *Do not overbake.* Place 1 chocolate kiss in center of each cookie. Cool 2 minutes on baking sheet. Remove cookies to foil to cool completely.

*Makes about 3 dozen cookies*

## RUGELACH

1½ cups all-purpose flour
¼ teaspoon salt
¼ teaspoon baking soda
½ cup butter, softened
1 package (3 ounces) cream cheese,
    softened
⅓ cup plus ¼ cup granulated sugar,
    divided
1 teaspoon grated lemon peel, divided
1 cup ground toasted walnuts
1 teaspoon ground cinnamon
2 tablespoons honey
1 tablespoon lemon juice
    Powdered sugar

**1.** Combine flour, salt and baking soda in small bowl.

**2.** Beat butter, cream cheese, ⅓ cup granulated sugar and ½ teaspoon lemon peel in large bowl with electric mixer at medium speed about 5 minutes or until light and fluffy. Gradually add flour mixture. Beat at low speed until well blended.

**3.** Form dough into three 5-inch discs; wrap in plastic wrap and refrigerate until firm, about 2 hours.

**4.** Preheat oven to 375°F. Grease cookie sheet; set aside.

**5.** Combine walnuts, remaining ¼ cup granulated sugar and cinnamon in medium bowl; set aside. Combine honey, remaining ½ teaspoon lemon peel and lemon juice in small bowl; set aside.

**6.** Working with 1 piece of dough at a time, place dough on lightly floured surface. Roll out with lightly floured rolling pin to 10-inch circle. Keep remaining dough refrigerated.

**7.** Brush with ⅓ of honey mixture. Sprinkle with ⅓ cup nut mixture. Lightly press nut mixture into dough.

**8.** Cut circle into 12 triangles with pizza cutter or sharp knife. Beginning with wide end of triangle, tightly roll up, jelly-roll fashion. Place cookies 1 inch apart on prepared cookie sheet.

**9.** Repeat with 2 remaining dough pieces and filling ingredients. Bake 10 to 12 minutes or until lightly golden brown. Let cookies stand on cookie sheets 1 minute. Remove cookies to wire rack; cool completely. Sprinkle with powdered sugar. Store tightly covered.

*Makes 3 dozen cookies*

**Note:** To toast walnuts, spread them in single layer on baking sheet; bake in preheated 350°F oven for 8 to 10 minutes or until golden brown, stirring frequently. Remove walnuts from baking sheet to cool. To grind walnuts, place in food processor. Process using on/off pulsing action until ground, but not pasty.

## CHOCOLATE TASSIES

2 cups all-purpose flour
2 packages (3 ounces each) cold cream cheese, cut into chunks
1 cup cold butter, cut into chunks
2 tablespoons butter
2 squares (1 ounce each) unsweetened chocolate
1½ cups packed brown sugar
2 eggs, beaten
2 teaspoons vanilla
Dash salt
1½ cups chopped pecans

Place flour in large bowl. Cut in cream cheese and cold butter. Continue to mix until dough can be shaped into ball. Wrap dough in plastic wrap; refrigerate 1 hour. Shape dough into 1-inch balls. Press each ball into ungreased miniature (1¾-inch) muffin pan cup, covering bottom and side of cup with dough.

Preheat oven to 350°F. Melt 2 tablespoons butter and chocolate in heavy medium saucepan over low heat. Remove from heat. Blend in brown sugar, eggs, vanilla and salt; beat until thick. Stir in pecans. Spoon about 1 teaspoon filling into each unbaked pastry shell. Bake 20 to 25 minutes or until pastry is lightly browned and filling is set. Cool in pans on wire racks. Remove from pans; store in airtight containers.

*Makes about 5 dozen cookies*

## TOFFEE SPATTERED SUGAR STARS

1¼ cups granulated sugar
  1 Butter Flavor* CRISCO® stick or 1 cup
      Butter Flavor* CRISCO® all-vegetable
      shortening
  2 eggs
  ¼ cup light corn syrup or regular pancake
      syrup
  1 tablespoon vanilla
  3 cups all-purpose flour (plus 4
      tablespoons), divided
  ¾ teaspoon baking powder
  ½ teaspoon baking soda
  ½ teaspoon salt
  1 package (6 ounces) milk chocolate
      English toffee chips, divided

*Butter Flavor Crisco® is artificially flavored.*

**1.** Place sugar and 1 cup shortening in large bowl. Beat at medium speed of electric mixer until well blended. Add eggs, syrup and vanilla; beat until well blended and fluffy.

**2.** Combine 3 cups flour, baking powder, baking soda and salt. Add gradually to shortening mixture, beating at low speed until well blended.

**3.** Divide dough into 4 equal pieces; shape each into disk. Wrap with plastic wrap. Refrigerate 1 hour or until firm.

**4.** Heat oven to 375°F. Place sheets of foil on countertop for cooling cookies.

**5.** Sprinkle about 1 tablespoon flour on large sheet of waxed paper. Place disk of dough on floured paper; flatten slightly with hands. Turn dough over; cover with another large sheet of waxed paper. Roll dough to ¼-inch thickness. Remove top sheet of waxed paper. Sprinkle about ¼ of toffee chips over dough. Roll lightly into dough. Cut out with floured star or round cookie cutter. Place 2 inches apart on ungreased baking sheet. Repeat with remaining dough and toffee chips.

**6.** Bake one baking sheet at a time at 375°F for 5 to 7 minutes or until cookies are lightly browned around edges. *Do not overbake.* Cool 2 minutes on baking sheet. Remove cookies to foil to cool completely.

*Makes about 3½ dozen cookies*

*When reusing cookie sheets for several batches of cookies, cool the sheets completely before placing dough on them. The dough will soften and begin to spread on a hot cookie sheet.*

*From top to bottom: Pecan Cookies (page 14) and Toffee Spattered Sugar Stars*

## PEEK–A–BOO APRICOT COOKIES

4 ounces bittersweet chocolate candy bar,
  broken into pieces
3 cups all-purpose flour
½ teaspoon baking soda
½ teaspoon salt
⅔ cup butter, softened
¾ cup sugar
2 large eggs
2 teaspoons vanilla
  Apricot preserves

1. Melt chocolate in small bowl set in bowl of very hot water, stirring twice. Combine flour, baking soda and salt in medium bowl.

2. Beat butter and sugar in large bowl with electric mixer at medium speed until light and fluffy. Beat in eggs, 1 at a time, beating well after each addition. Beat in vanilla and chocolate. Beat in flour mixture at low speed until well blended.

3. Divide dough into 2 rounds; flatten into discs. Wrap in plastic wrap; refrigerate 2 hours or until firm.

4. Preheat oven to 350°F.

5. Roll out dough on lightly floured surface to ¼- to ⅛-inch thickness. Cut out rounds with 2½-inch cutter. Cut 1-inch centers out of half the rounds. Reserve scraps. Place rounds on ungreased cookie sheets. Repeat rolling and cutting with remaining scraps of dough.

6. Bake cookies 9 to 10 minutes or until set. Let cookies stand on cookie sheets 2 minutes. Remove cookies with spatula to wire rack; cool completely.

7. To assemble cookies, spread about 1½ teaspoons preserves over flat side of cookie circles; top with cut-out cookies to form a sandwich.

8. Store tightly covered at room temperature. These cookies do not freeze well.
*Makes about 1½ dozen cookies*

## HERSHEY'S MINT CHOCOLATE COOKIES

¾ cup (1½ sticks) butter or margarine,
  softened
1 cup sugar
1 egg
1 teaspoon vanilla extract
1½ cups all-purpose flour
½ teaspoon baking soda
¼ teaspoon salt
1⅔ cups (10-ounce package) HERSHEY'S
  Mint Chocolate Chips

1. Heat oven to 350°F.

2. In large bowl, beat butter and sugar until light and fluffy. Add egg and vanilla; beat well. Stir together flour, baking soda and salt; gradually blend into butter mixture. Stir in chocolate chips. Drop by rounded teaspoonfuls onto ungreased cookie sheet.

3. Bake 8 to 9 minutes or just until lightly browned. Cool slightly; remove from cookie sheet to wire rack. Cool completely.
*Makes about 2½ dozen cookies*

*Peek-a-Boo Apricot Cookies*

## ORANGE–CARDAMOM THINS

1¼ cups granulated sugar
  1 Butter Flavor* CRISCO® Stick or 1 cup
    Butter Flavor* CRISCO® all-vegetable
    shortening plus additional for
    greasing
  1 egg
  ¼ cup light corn syrup or regular pancake
    syrup
  1 teaspoon vanilla
  1 tablespoon grated orange peel
  ½ teaspoon orange extract
  3 cups all-purpose flour
1¼ teaspoons cardamom
  ¾ teaspoon baking powder
  ½ teaspoon baking soda
  ½ teaspoon salt
  ½ teaspoon cinnamon

*Butter Flavor Crisco® is artificially flavored.*

**1.** Place sugar and 1 cup shortening in large
bowl. Beat at medium speed of electric mixer
until well blended. Add egg, syrup, vanilla,
orange peel and orange extract; beat until
well blended and fluffy.

**2.** Combine flour, cardamom, baking powder,
baking soda, salt and cinnamon. Add
gradually to shortening mixture, beating at
low speed until well blended.

**3.** Divide dough in half. Roll each half into
12-inch-long log. Wrap with plastic wrap.
Refrigerate for 4 hours or until firm.

**4.** Heat oven to 375°F. Grease baking sheets.
Place sheets of foil on countertop for cooling
cookies.

**5.** Cut rolls into ¼-inch-thick slices. Place
1 inch apart on prepared baking sheets.

**6.** Bake one baking sheet at a time at 375°F
for 7 to 9 minutes or until bottoms of cookies
are lightly browned. *Do not overbake.* Cool
2 minutes on baking sheet. Remove cookies
to foil to cool completely.

*Makes about 5 dozen cookies*

## ALMOND LACE COOKIES

  ¼ cup butter, softened
  ½ cup sugar
  ½ cup BLUE DIAMOND® Blanched
    Almond Paste
  ¼ cup all-purpose flour
  ¼ teaspoon salt
  ½ teaspoon almond extract
  2 tablespoons milk
  2 teaspoons grated orange peel

Cream butter and sugar. Beat in almond
paste. Add remaining ingredients. Mix well.
Drop rounded teaspoonfuls onto cookie
sheet, 3 inches apart. (Cookies will spread.)
Bake at 350°F for 8 to 10 minutes or until
edges are lightly browned. Cool 3 to 4
minutes on cookie sheet; remove and cool on
wire rack. *Makes 1½ dozen cookies*

## DOUBLE–DIPPED HAZELNUT CRISPS

¾ cup semisweet chocolate chips
1¼ cups all-purpose flour
¾ cup powdered sugar
⅔ cup whole hazelnuts, toasted, skinned
   and ground*
¼ teaspoon instant espresso powder
   Dash salt
½ cup butter, softened
2 teaspoons vanilla
4 squares (1 ounce each) bittersweet or
   semisweet chocolate
2 teaspoons shortening, divided
4 ounces white chocolate

*To grind hazelnuts, place in food processor or blender. Process until thoroughly ground with a dry, not pasty, texture.*

Preheat oven to 350°F. Lightly grease cookie sheets or line with parchment paper. Melt chocolate chips in top of double boiler over hot, not boiling, water. Remove from heat; cool. Blend flour, sugar, hazelnuts, espresso powder and salt in large bowl. Blend in butter, melted chocolate and vanilla until dough is stiff but smooth. (If dough is too soft to handle, cover and refrigerate until firm.)

Roll out dough, ¼ at a time, to ⅛-inch thickness on lightly floured surface. Cut out with 2-inch scalloped round cutters. Place 2 inches apart on prepared cookie sheets. Bake 8 minutes or until not quite firm. (Cookies should not brown. They will puff up during baking and then fall again.) Remove to wire racks to cool.

Place bittersweet chocolate and 1 teaspoon shortening in small bowl. Place bowl over hot water; stir until chocolate is melted and smooth. Dip cookies, 1 at a time, halfway into bittersweet chocolate. Place on waxed paper; refrigerate until chocolate is set. Repeat melting process with white chocolate. Dip other halves of cookies into white chocolate; refrigerate until set. Store cookies in airtight container in cool place. (If cookies are frozen, chocolate may discolor.)

*Makes about 4 dozen cookies*

*To melt chocolate in a microwave oven, place 2 unwrapped squares or 1 cup chips in a microwavable bowl. Microwave at HIGH for 1 to 1½ minutes, stirring after 1 minute. Be sure to stir chocolate since it may retain its original shape even when melted.*

## ORANGE & CHOCOLATE RIBBON COOKIES

1 cup (2 sticks) butter, softened
½ cup sugar
3 egg yolks
2 teaspoons grated orange peel
1 teaspoon orange extract
2¼ cups all-purpose flour, divided
3 tablespoons unsweetened cocoa powder
1 teaspoon vanilla
1 teaspoon chocolate extract

Beat butter, sugar and egg yolks in large bowl until light and fluffy. Remove half of mixture; place in another bowl. Add orange peel, orange extract and 1¼ cups of the flour to one bowl; mix until blended and smooth. Shape into a ball. Add cocoa, vanilla and chocolate extract to remaining mixture; beat until smooth. Stir in remaining 1 cup flour; mix until blended and smooth. Shape into a ball. Cover dough; refrigerate 10 minutes.

Roll out each dough separately on lightly floured surface to 12×4-inch rectangle. Pat edges of dough to straighten; use rolling pin to level off thickness. Place one dough on top of the other. Using sharp knife, make lengthwise cut through center of doughs. Lift half of dough onto other to make long, 4-layer strip of dough. With hands, press dough strips together. Wrap in plastic wrap; refrigerate at least 1 hour or up to 3 days.

Preheat oven to 350°F. Grease cookie sheets. Cut dough crosswise into ¼-inch-thick slices; place 2 inches apart on prepared cookie sheets. Bake 10 to 12 minutes or until very lightly browned. Remove to wire racks to cool. *Makes about 5 dozen cookies*

## MARVELOUS MACAROONS

1 can (8 ounces) DOLE® Crushed Pineapple
1 can (14 ounces) sweetened condensed milk
1 package (7 ounces) flaked coconut
½ cup margarine, melted
½ cup DOLE® Chopped Almonds, toasted
1 teaspoon grated lemon peel
¼ teaspoon almond extract
1 cup all-purpose flour
1 teaspoon baking powder

• Preheat oven to 350°F. Drain pineapple well, pressing out excess juice with back of spoon. In large bowl, combine drained pineapple, milk, coconut, margarine, almonds, lemon peel and almond extract.

• In small bowl, combine flour and baking powder. Beat into pineapple mixture until blended. Drop heaping tablespoonfuls of dough 1 inch apart onto greased cookie sheets.

• Bake 13 to 15 minutes or until lightly browned. Garnish with whole almonds, if desired. Cool on wire racks. Store in covered container in refrigerator.
*Makes about 3½ dozen cookies*

*Marvelous Macaroons*

## BLACK FOREST OATMEAL FANCIES

1 cup Butter Flavor* CRISCO®
  all-vegetable shortening
1 cup firmly packed brown sugar
1 cup granulated sugar
2 eggs
2 teaspoons vanilla
1⅔ cups all-purpose flour
1 teaspoon baking soda
1 teaspoon salt
½ teaspoon baking powder
3 cups quick oats (not instant or old
  fashioned), uncooked
1 baking bar (6 ounces) white chocolate,
  coarsely chopped
6 squares (1 ounce each) semisweet
  chocolate, coarsely chopped
½ cup coarsely chopped red candied
  cherries
½ cup sliced almonds

*Butter Flavor Crisco® is artificially flavored.*

**1.** Heat oven to 375°F. Place foil on countertop for cooling cookies. Combine 1 cup shortening, brown sugar, granulated sugar, eggs and vanilla in large bowl. Beat at medium speed of electric mixer until well blended.

**2.** Combine flour, baking soda, salt and baking powder. Mix into shortening mixture at low speed until well blended. Stir in, one at a time, oats, white chocolate, semi-sweet chocolate, cherries and almonds with spoon.

**3.** Drop rounded tablespoonfuls of dough 2 inches apart onto ungreased baking sheets.

**4.** Bake at 375°F for 9 to 11 minutes or until set. Cool 2 minutes on baking sheets. Remove cookies to foil to cool completely.

*Makes about 3 dozen cookies*

## CHOCOLATE PISTACHIO FINGERS

¾ cup butter, softened
⅓ cup sugar
3 ounces (about ⅓ cup) almond paste
1 egg yolk
1⅔ cups all-purpose flour
1 cup (6 ounces) semisweet chocolate
  chips
½ cup finely chopped natural pistachios

Preheat oven to 350°F. Line cookie sheets with parchment paper or lightly grease and dust with flour.

Beat butter and sugar in large bowl until blended. Add almond paste and egg yolk; beat until light. Blend in flour to make a smooth dough. (If dough is too soft to handle, cover and refrigerate until firm.) Turn out onto lightly floured surface. Divide into 8 equal pieces; divide each piece in half. Roll each half into 12-inch rope; cut each rope into 2-inch lengths. Place 2 inches apart on prepared cookie sheets.

Bake 10 to 12 minutes or until edges just begin to brown. Remove to wire racks to cool. Melt chocolate chips in small bowl over hot water. Stir until smooth. Dip both ends of cookies about ½ inch into melted chocolate; dip chocolate ends into pistachios. Place on waxed paper; let stand until chocolate is set.

*Makes 8 dozen cookies*

## WELSH TEA CAKES

¾ cup chopped dried mixed fruit or fruit
  bits or golden raisins
2 tablespoons brandy or cognac
2¼ cups all-purpose flour
2½ teaspoons cinnamon, divided
1 teaspoon baking powder
½ teaspoon baking soda
¼ teaspoon salt
¼ teaspoon ground cloves
1 cup butter, softened
1¼ cups granulated sugar, divided
1 large egg
  Additional granulated sugar
⅓ cup sliced almonds (optional)

1. Preheat oven to 375°F. Combine dried fruit and brandy in medium bowl; let sit at least 10 minutes to plump.

2. Place flour, 1½ teaspoons cinnamon, baking powder, baking soda, salt and cloves in medium bowl; stir to combine.

3. Beat butter and 1 cup sugar in large bowl with electric mixer at medium speed until light and fluffy. Beat in egg. Gradually add flour. Beat at low speed until well blended. Stir in fruit mixture.

4. Combine remaining ¼ cup sugar and 1 teaspoon cinnamon in small bowl. Roll heaping teaspoonfuls of dough into 1-inch balls; roll balls in cinnamon sugar to coat. Place balls 2 inches apart on ungreased cookie sheets.

5. Press balls to ¼-inch thickness using bottom of glass dipped in granulated sugar. Press 3 almond slices into each cookie.

6. Bake 10 to 12 minutes or until lightly browned. Remove to wire racks; cool completely.   *Makes about 3½ dozen cookies*

## PHILLY® APRICOT COOKIES

1½ cups butter or margarine, softened
1½ cups granulated sugar
1 (8-ounce) package PHILADELPHIA®
  Cream Cheese, softened
2 eggs
1½ teaspoons grated lemon peel
2 tablespoons lemon juice
4½ cups all-purpose flour
1½ teaspoons baking powder
  KRAFT® Apricot Preserves
  Powdered sugar

• Combine butter, granulated sugar and cream cheese in large bowl, mixing until well blended. Blend in eggs, peel and juice. Add combined flour and baking powder; mix well. Cover; refrigerate several hours.

• Preheat oven to 350°F.

• Shape level measuring tablespoonfuls of dough into balls. Place on ungreased cookie sheet; flatten slightly. Indent centers; fill with preserves.

• Bake 15 minutes or until lightly browned. Cool on wire rack; sprinkle with powdered sugar.   *Makes about 7 dozen cookies*

## CHOCOLATE SURPRISE COOKIES

2¾ cups all-purpose flour
¾ cup unsweetened cocoa powder
½ teaspoon baking powder
½ teaspoon baking soda
1 cup (2 sticks) butter, softened
1½ cups packed light brown sugar
½ cup plus 1 tablespoon granulated sugar, divided
2 eggs
1 teaspoon vanilla
1 cup chopped pecans, divided
1 package (9 ounces) caramels coated in milk chocolate
3 squares (1 ounce each) white chocolate, coarsely chopped

Preheat oven to 375°F. Combine flour, cocoa, baking powder and baking soda in medium bowl; set aside.

Beat butter, brown sugar and ½ cup granulated sugar with electric mixer at medium speed until light and fluffy; beat in eggs and vanilla. Gradually add flour mixture and ½ cup pecans; beat well. Cover dough; refrigerate 15 minutes or until firm enough to roll into balls.

Place remaining ½ cup pecans and 1 tablespoon sugar in shallow dish. Roll tablespoonful of dough around 1 caramel candy, covering completely; press one side into nut mixture. Place, nut side up, on ungreased cookie sheet. Repeat with additional dough and candies, placing 3 inches apart.

Bake 10 to 12 minutes or until set and slightly cracked. Let stand on cookie sheet 2 minutes. Transfer cookies to wire rack; cool completely.

Place white chocolate pieces in small resealable plastic freezer bag; seal bag. Microwave at MEDIUM (50% power) 2 minutes. Turn bag over; microwave 2 to 3 minutes or until melted. Knead bag until chocolate is smooth. Cut off tiny corner of bag; drizzle chocolate onto cookies. Let stand about 30 minutes or until chocolate is set.

*Makes about 3½ dozen cookies*

*Cooling cookies for a minute or two on cookie sheets allows them to set. Otherwise they may be too tender to move right out of the oven.*

*Chocolate Surprise Cookies*

## MORAVIAN SPICE CRISPS

⅓ **cup shortening**
⅓ **cup packed brown sugar**
¼ **cup unsulfured molasses**
¼ **cup dark corn syrup**
1¾ **to 2 cups all-purpose flour**
2 **teaspoons ground ginger**
1¼ **teaspoons baking soda**
1 **teaspoon ground cinnamon**
½ **teaspoon ground cloves**
**Powdered sugar**

**1.** Melt shortening in small saucepan over low heat. Remove from heat; stir in brown sugar, molasses and corn syrup. Set aside; cool.

**2.** Place 1½ cups flour, ginger, baking soda, cinnamon and cloves in large bowl; stir to combine. Beat in shortening mixture with electric mixer at medium speed. Gradually beat in additional flour until stiff dough forms.

**3.** Knead dough on lightly floured surface, adding more flour if too sticky. Form dough into 2 discs; wrap in plastic wrap and refrigerate 30 minutes or until firm.

**4.** Preheat oven to 350°F. Grease cookie sheets; set aside. Working with 1 disc at a time, roll out dough on lightly floured surface to 1/16-inch thickness.

**5.** Cut dough with floured 2⅜-inch scalloped cookie cutter. (If dough becomes too soft, refrigerate several minutes before continuing.) Gently press dough trimmings together; reroll and cut out more cookies. Place cookies ½ inch apart on prepared cookie sheets.

**6.** Bake 8 minutes or until firm and lightly browned. Remove cookies with spatula to wire racks; cool completely.

**7.** Place small strips of cardboard or parchment paper over cookies; dust with sifted powdered sugar. Carefully remove cardboard. *Makes about 6 dozen cookies*

## GREEK LEMON–HERB COOKIES

2½ **cups all-purpose flour**
1 **teaspoon baking soda**
¼ **teaspoon salt**
1 **cup butter, softened**
1¼ **cups sugar, divided**
2 **large eggs, separated**
4 **teaspoons grated lemon peel, divided**
½ **teaspoon dried rosemary leaves, crushed**

**1.** Preheat oven to 375°F. Place flour, baking soda and salt in large bowl; stir to combine.

**2.** Beat butter and 1 cup sugar in large bowl with electric mixer at medium speed until light and fluffy. Beat in egg yolks, 3 teaspoons lemon peel and rosemary. Gradually add flour mixture. Beat at low speed until well blended.

**3.** Combine remaining ¼ cup sugar and 1 teaspoon lemon peel in small bowl.

**4.** Roll tablespoonfuls of dough into 1-inch balls; roll in sugar mixture to coat.

**5.** Place balls 2 inches apart on *ungreased* cookie sheets. Press balls to ¼-inch thickness using flat bottom of drinking glass.

**6.** Bake 10 to 12 minutes or until edges are golden brown. Remove cookies to wire racks; cool completely.

**7.** Store tightly covered at room temperature or freeze up to 3 months.

*Makes about 4 dozen cookies*

*Moravian Spice Crisps*

# DELICIOUSLY EASY

## CHOCO–COCO PECAN CRISPS

½ cup butter, softened
1 cup packed light brown sugar
1 egg
1 teaspoon vanilla
1½ cups all-purpose flour
1 cup chopped pecans
⅓ cup unsweetened cocoa
½ teaspoon baking soda
1 cup flaked coconut

Cream butter and sugar in large bowl until light and fluffy. Beat in egg and vanilla. Combine flour, pecans, cocoa and baking soda in small bowl until well blended. Add to creamed mixture, blending until stiff dough is formed. Sprinkle coconut on work surface. Divide dough into 4 parts. Shape each part into a roll about 1½ inches in diameter; roll in coconut until thickly coated. Wrap in plastic wrap; refrigerate until firm, at least 1 hour or up to 2 weeks.

Preheat oven to 350°F. Cut rolls into ⅛-inch-thick slices. Place 2 inches apart on ungreased cookie sheets. Bake 10 to 13 minutes or until firm, but not overly browned. Remove to wire racks to cool.

*Makes about 6 dozen cookies*

*Choco-Coco Pecan Crisps*

## CHEWY LEMON–HONEY COOKIES

**2 cups all-purpose flour**
**1½ teaspoons baking soda**
**½ cup honey**
**⅓ cup FLEISCHMANN'S® Original Margarine**
**¼ cup granulated sugar**
**1 tablespoon grated lemon peel**
**¼ cup EGG BEATERS® Healthy Real Egg Substitute**
**Lemon Glaze, optional (recipe follows)**

In small bowl, combine flour and baking soda; set aside.

In large bowl, with electric mixer at medium speed, beat honey, margarine, granulated sugar and lemon peel until creamy. Add Egg Beaters; beat until smooth. Gradually stir in flour mixture until blended.

Drop dough by rounded teaspoonfuls, 2 inches apart, onto lightly greased baking sheets. Bake at 350°F for 7 to 8 minutes or until lightly browned. Remove from sheets; cool completely on wire racks. Drizzle with Lemon Glaze if desired.

*Makes 3½ dozen cookies*

**Lemon Glaze:** In small bowl, combine 1 cup powdered sugar and 2 tablespoons lemon juice until smooth.

**Prep Time:** 20 minutes
**Cook Time:** 8 minutes

## PEANUT BUTTER CHOCOLATE STARS

**1 cup peanut butter**
**1 cup packed light brown sugar**
**1 egg**
**24 milk chocolate candy stars or other solid milk chocolate candy**

Preheat oven to 350°F. Combine peanut butter, sugar and egg in medium bowl until blended and smooth.

Shape dough into 24 balls about 1½ inches in diameter. Place 2 inches apart on ungreased cookie sheets. Press one chocolate star on top of each cookie. Bake 10 to 12 minutes or until set. Transfer to wire racks to cool completely.

*Makes about 2 dozen cookies*

*Peanut butter and chocolate are a delightful combination in these super-easy flourless cookies.*

*Peanut Butter Chocolate Stars*

## CHEWY CHOCOLATE NO–BAKES

1 cup (6 ounces) semisweet chocolate pieces
16 large marshmallows
⅓ cup (5 tablespoons plus 1 teaspoon) margarine or butter
2 cups QUAKER® Oats (quick or old fashioned, uncooked)
1 cup (any combination of) raisins, diced dried mixed fruit, flaked coconut, miniature marshmallows or chopped nuts
1 teaspoon vanilla

In large saucepan over low heat, melt chocolate pieces, marshmallows and margarine, stirring until smooth. Remove from heat; cool slightly. Stir in remaining ingredients. Drop by rounded teaspoonfuls onto wax paper. Chill 2 to 3 hours. Let stand at room temperature about 15 minutes before serving. Store in tightly covered container in refrigerator.        *Makes 3 dozen cookies*

**Microwave Directions:** Place chocolate pieces, marshmallows and margarine in large microwavable bowl. Microwave on HIGH 1 to 2 minutes or until mixture is melted and smooth, stirring every 30 seconds. Proceed as recipe directs.

## FRUIT BURST COOKIES

1 cup margarine or butter, softened
¼ cup sugar
1 teaspoon almond extract
2 cups all-purpose flour
½ teaspoon salt
1 cup finely chopped nuts
  SMUCKER'S® Simply Fruit

Beat margarine and sugar until light and fluffy. Blend in almond extract. Combine flour and salt; add to mixture and blend well. Shape level tablespoonfuls of dough into balls; roll in nuts. Place 2 inches apart on ungreased cookie sheets; flatten slightly. Indent centers; fill with fruit spread. Bake at 400°F for 10 to 12 minutes or just until lightly browned. Cool.        *Makes 2½ dozen cookies*

## CHOCOLATE CANDY COOKIES

⅔ cup MIRACLE WHIP® Salad Dressing
1 two-layer devil's food cake mix
2 eggs
1 (8-ounce) package candy-coated chocolate candies

• Preheat oven to 375°F.

• Blend salad dressing, cake mix and eggs at low speed with electric mixer until moistened. Beat on medium speed 2 minutes. Stir in chocolate candies. (Dough will be stiff.)

• Drop by rounded teaspoonfuls, 2 inches apart, onto greased cookie sheets.

• Bake 9 to 11 minutes or until almost set. (Cookies will still appear soft.) Cool 1 minute; remove from cookie sheets.
        *Makes about 4½ dozen cookies*

## LEMON COOKIES

⅔ cup **MIRACLE WHIP® Salad Dressing**
 1 **two-layer yellow cake mix**
 2 **eggs**
 2 **teaspoons grated lemon peel**
⅔ cup **ready-to-spread vanilla frosting**
 4 **teaspoons lemon juice**

• Preheat oven to 375°F.

• Blend salad dressing, cake mix and eggs at low speed with electric mixer until moistened. Add peel. Beat on medium speed 2 minutes. (Dough will be stiff.)

• Drop rounded teaspoonfuls of dough, 2 inches apart, onto greased cookie sheet.

• Bake 9 to 11 minutes or until lightly browned. (Cookies will still appear soft.) Cool 1 minute; remove from cookie sheet. Cool completely on wire rack.

• Stir together frosting and juice until well blended. Spread on cookies.

*Makes about 4 dozen cookies*

## PEANUT BUTTER & JELLY COOKIES

 1 **package DUNCAN HINES® Peanut Butter Cookie Mix**
¾ cup **quick-cooking oats (not instant or old-fashioned)**
 1 **egg**
¼ cup **canola oil**
½ cup **grape jelly**
½ cup **confectioners' sugar**
 2 **teaspoons water**

**1.** Preheat oven to 375°F.

**2.** Combine cookie mix, oats, egg and oil in large bowl. Stir until well blended. Divide dough into 4 equal portions. Shape each portion into 12-inch-long log on waxed paper. Place logs on ungreased cookie sheets. Press back of spoon down center of each log to form indentation. Bake at 375°F for 10 to 12 minutes or until light golden brown. Press back of spoon down center of each log again. Let stand 2 minutes on cookie sheets. Remove to cooling racks. Cool completely. Spoon 2 tablespoons jelly along indentation of each log.

**3.** Combine confectioners' sugar and water in small bowl. Stir until smooth. Drizzle over each log. Allow glaze to set. Cut each log diagonally into 12 slices with large, sharp knife. Store between layers of waxed paper in airtight container. *Makes about 48 cookies*

## ORANGE PECAN REFRIGERATOR COOKIES

2⅓ cups all-purpose flour
½ teaspoon baking soda
¼ teaspoon salt
½ cup butter or margarine, softened
½ cup packed brown sugar
½ cup granulated sugar
1 egg, lightly beaten
 Grated peel of 1 SUNKIST® Orange
3 tablespoons fresh squeezed orange juice
¾ cup pecan pieces

In bowl, stir together flour, baking soda and salt. In large bowl, blend together butter, brown sugar and granulated sugar. Add egg, orange peel and juice; beat well. Stir in pecans. Gradually beat in flour mixture. (Dough will be stiff.) Divide mixture in half and shape each half (on long piece of waxed paper) into roll about 1¼ inches in diameter and 12 inches long. Roll up tightly in waxed paper. Chill several hours or overnight.

Cut into ¼-inch slices and arrange on lightly greased cookie sheets. Bake at 350°F for 10 to 12 minutes or until lightly browned. Cool on wire racks.       *Makes about 6 dozen cookies*

**Chocolate Filled Sandwich Cookies:** Cut each roll into ⅛-inch slices and bake as above. When cool, to make each sandwich cookie, spread about 1 teaspoon canned chocolate fudge frosting on bottom side of 1 cookie; cover with second cookie of same shape. Makes about 4 dozen double cookies.

## FUDGY PEANUT BUTTER JIFFY COOKIES

2 cups granulated sugar
½ cup evaporated milk
½ cup (1 stick) margarine or butter
¼ cup unsweetened cocoa powder
2½ cups QUAKER® Oats (quick or old fashioned, uncooked)
½ cup peanut butter
½ cup raisins or chopped dates
2 teaspoons vanilla

In large saucepan, combine sugar, milk, margarine and cocoa. Bring to boil over medium heat, stirring frequently. Continue boiling 3 minutes. Remove from heat. Stir in oats, peanut butter, raisins and vanilla; mix well. Quickly drop by tablespoonfuls onto waxed paper or greased cookie sheet. Let stand until set. Store tightly covered at room temperature.       *Makes about 3 dozen cookies*

## TOFFEE CREME SANDWICH COOKIES

**1 jar (7 ounces) marshmallow creme**
**¼ cup toffee baking chips**
**48 (2-inch) sugar or fudge-striped**
   **shortbread cookies**
   **Red and green jimmies**

**1.** Combine marshmallow creme and toffee chips in medium bowl until well blended. (Mixture will be stiff.)

**2.** Spread 1 teaspoon of marshmallow mixture on bottom of 1 cookie; top with bottom side of another cookie. Roll side of sandwich cookie in jimmies. Repeat with remaining marshmallow creme mixture, cookies and jimmies.    *Makes 2 dozen cookies*

**Prep Time:** 20 minutes

*Toffee Creme Sandwich Cookies*

## 3–MINUTE NO–BAKE COOKIES

**2 cups granulated sugar**
**½ cup 2% low-fat milk**
**½ cup (1 stick) margarine or butter**
**⅓ cup unsweetened cocoa powder**
**3 cups QUAKER® Oats (quick or old fashioned, uncooked)**

In large saucepan, combine sugar, milk, margarine and cocoa. Bring to boil over medium heat, stirring frequently. Continue boiling 3 minutes. Remove from heat. Stir in oats; mix well. Quickly drop by tablespoonfuls onto waxed paper or greased cookie sheet. Let stand until set. Store tightly covered at room temperature.

*Makes about 3 dozen cookies*

## BANANA ENERGY BALLS

**1 extra-ripe, medium DOLE® Banana**
**¼ cup peanut butter**
**¼ cup semisweet chocolate chips**
**2 tablespoons honey**
**1⅓ cups natural wheat and barley cereal**
**⅓ cup finely chopped peanuts**

• Mash banana with fork. Measure ½ cup.

• Combine banana, peanut butter and chocolate chips.

• Heat honey in microwave for 15 seconds or until hot. Add to banana mixture; stir 30 seconds. Add cereal; mix well. Cover; set aside for 30 minutes.

• Form balls using 1 tablespoon mixture, then roll in peanuts. Store in airtight container.

*Makes 20 servings*

## QUICK CHOCOLATE SOFTIES

**1 package (18.25 ounces) devil's food cake mix**
**⅓ cup water**
**¼ cup butter, softened**
**1 egg**
**1 cup white chocolate baking chips**
**½ cup coarsely chopped walnuts**

Preheat oven to 350°F. Grease cookie sheets. Combine cake mix, water, butter and egg in large bowl. Beat with electric mixer at low speed until moistened, scraping down side of bowl once. Increase speed to medium; beat 1 minute. (Dough will be thick.) Stir in chips and nuts; mix until well blended. Drop dough by heaping teaspoonfuls 2 inches apart onto prepared cookie sheets.

Bake 10 to 12 minutes or until set. Let cookies stand on cookie sheets 1 minute. Remove cookies to wire racks; cool completely.

*Makes about 4 dozen cookies*

*Quick Chocolate Softies*

# NOT JUST FOR KIDS

## KIDS' FAVORITE JUMBO CHIPPERS

1 cup butter, softened
¾ cup granulated sugar
¾ cup packed brown sugar
2 eggs
1 teaspoon vanilla
2¼ cups all-purpose flour
1 teaspoon baking soda
¾ teaspoon salt
1 package (9 ounces) candy-coated chocolate pieces
1 cup peanut butter flavored chips

Preheat oven to 375°F. Beat butter, granulated sugar and brown sugar in large bowl until light and fluffy. Beat in eggs and vanilla. Add flour, baking soda and salt. Beat until well blended. Stir in chocolate pieces and peanut butter chips. Drop by rounded tablespoonfuls 3 inches apart onto ungreased cookie sheets. Bake 10 to 12 minutes or until edges are golden brown. Let cookies stand on cookie sheets 2 minutes. Remove cookies to wire racks; cool completely.                     *Makes 3 dozen cookies*

**Note:** For a change of pace, substitute white chocolate chips, chocolate chips, chocolate-covered raisins, toffee bits or any of your cookie monsters' favorite candy pieces for the candy-coated chocolate pieces.

*Kids' Favorite Jumbo Chippers*

## SMUSHY COOKIES

**COOKIES**
**1 package (20 ounces) refrigerated cookie dough, any flavor**
**All-purpose flour (optional)**

**FILLINGS**
**Peanut butter, multi-colored miniature marshmallows, assorted colored sprinkles, chocolate-covered raisins and caramel candy squares**

**1.** Preheat oven to 350°F. Grease cookie sheets.

**2.** Remove dough from wrapper according to package directions. Cut into 4 equal sections. Reserve 1 section; refrigerate remaining 3 sections.

**3.** Roll reserved dough to ¼-inch thickness. Sprinkle with flour to minimize sticking, if necessary. Cut out cookies using 2½-inch round cookie cutter. Transfer to prepared cookie sheets. Repeat with remaining dough, working with 1 section at a time.

**4.** Bake 8 to 11 minutes or until edges are light golden brown. Remove to wire racks; cool completely.

**5.** To make sandwich, spread about 1½ tablespoons peanut butter on underside of 1 cookie to within ¼ inch of edge. Sprinkle with miniature marshmallows and candy pieces. Top with second cookie, pressing gently. Repeat with remaining cookies and fillings.

**6.** Just before serving, place sandwiches on paper towels. Microwave on HIGH (100%) 15 to 25 seconds or until fillings become soft.
*Makes about 8 to 10 sandwich cookies*

## CRUNCHY CHOCOLATE CHIPSTERS

**½ Butter Flavor\* CRISCO® Stick or ½ cup Butter Flavor\* CRISCO® all-vegetable shortening plus additional for greasing**
**½ cup firmly packed brown sugar**
**½ cup granulated sugar**
**2 tablespoons milk**
**1 egg**
**1 teaspoon vanilla**
**1¼ cups all-purpose flour**
**½ teaspoon baking soda**
**¼ teaspoon salt**
**2 cups crispy rice cereal**
**1 cup semisweet miniature chocolate chips**

*\*Butter Flavor Crisco® is artificially flavored.*

**1.** Preheat oven to 350°F. Grease cookie sheets with shortening. Place sheets of foil on countertop for cooling cookies.

**2.** Combine ½ cup shortening, brown sugar, granulated sugar and milk in large bowl. Beat at medium speed of electric mixer until well blended. Beat in egg and vanilla.

**3.** Combine flour, baking soda and salt. Mix into shortening mixture at low speed until blended. Stir in cereal and chocolate chips. Drop by level measuring tablespoonfuls 2 inches apart onto prepared baking sheets.

**4.** Bake at 350°F for 9 to 11 minutes or until set. *Do not overbake.* Cool 2 minutes on baking sheet. Remove cookies to foil to cool completely. *Makes about 4 dozen cookies*

*Smushy Cookies*

## ANGEL PILLOWS

½ **Butter Flavor\* CRISCO® Stick or ½ cup Butter Flavor\* CRISCO® all-vegetable shortening plus additional for greasing**
1 **package (3 ounces) cream cheese, softened**
1 **tablespoon milk**
¼ **cup firmly packed brown sugar**
½ **cup apricot preserves**
1¼ **cups all-purpose flour**
1½ **teaspoons baking powder**
1½ **teaspoons ground cinnamon**
¼ **teaspoon salt**
½ **cup coarsely chopped pecans or flake coconut**

### FROSTING
1 **cup confectioners' sugar**
¼ **cup apricot preserves**
1 **tablespoon Butter Flavor\* CRISCO® Stick or 1 tablespoon Butter Flavor\* CRISCO® all-vegetable shortening**
**Flake coconut or finely chopped pecans (optional)**

*\*Butter Flavor Crisco® is artificially flavored.*

Heat oven to 350°F. Grease baking sheets with shortening. Place sheets of foil on countertop for cooling cookies. Cream ½ cup shortening, cream cheese and milk at medium speed of electric mixer until well blended. Beat in brown sugar. Beat in preserves. Combine flour, baking powder, cinnamon and salt. Mix into creamed mixture. Stir in nuts. Drop 2 level measuring tablespoons of dough into a mound to form each cookie. Place 2 inches apart on baking sheets.

Bake one baking sheet at a time at 350°F for 14 minutes. *Do not overbake.* Cool on baking sheet one minute. Remove cookies to foil to cool completely.

For frosting, combine confectioners' sugar, preserves and shortening in small mixing bowl. Beat with electric mixer until well blended. Frost cooled cookies. Sprinkle coconut over frosting, if desired.

*Makes 1½ dozen cookies*

**Tip:** Try peach or pineapple preserves in place of apricot.

**Prep Time:** 25 minutes
**Bake Time:** 14 minutes

*Never store two different kinds of cookies in the same container because their flavors and textures can change.*

## QUICK PEANUT BUTTER CHOCOLATE CHIP COOKIES

**1 package DUNCAN HINES® Moist Deluxe Yellow Cake Mix**
**½ cup creamy peanut butter**
**½ cup butter or margarine, softened**
**2 eggs**
**1 cup milk chocolate chips**

**1.** Preheat oven to 350°F. Grease cookie sheets.

**2.** Combine cake mix, peanut butter, butter and eggs in large bowl. Mix at low speed with electric mixer until blended. Stir in chocolate chips.

**3.** Drop by rounded teaspoonfuls onto prepared cookie sheets. Bake 9 to 11 minutes or until lightly browned. Cool 2 minutes on cookie sheets. Remove to cooling racks.

*Makes about 4 dozen cookies*

**Tip:** Crunchy peanut butter may be substituted for regular peanut butter.

*Angel Pillow*

## SPICY GINGERBREAD COOKIES

**COOKIES**
- ¾ cup (1½ sticks) butter, softened
- ⅔ cup light molasses
- ½ cup firmly packed brown sugar
- 1 egg
- 1½ teaspoons grated lemon peel
- 2½ cups all-purpose flour
- 1¼ teaspoons ground cinnamon
- 1 teaspoon ground allspice
- 1 teaspoon vanilla
- ½ teaspoon baking soda
- ½ teaspoon salt
- ½ teaspoon ground ginger
- ¼ teaspoon baking powder

**FROSTING**
- 4 cups powdered sugar
- ½ cup (1 stick) butter, softened
- 4 tablespoons milk
- 2 teaspoons vanilla

For cookies, combine butter, molasses, brown sugar, egg and lemon peel in large bowl. Beat at medium speed until smooth and creamy. Add all remaining cookie ingredients. Reduce speed to low; beat well. Cover; refrigerate at least 2 hours.

Preheat oven to 350°F. Roll out dough, one half at a time, on well floured surface to ¼-inch thickness. (Keeping remaining dough refrigerated.) Cut out dough with 3- to 4-inch cookie cutters. Place on greased cookie sheets. Bake 6 to 8 minutes or until no indentation remains when touched. Remove immediately. Cool.

For frosting, combine powdered sugar, butter, milk and vanilla in small bowl. Beat at low speed until fluffy. Frost cookies.

*Makes about 4 dozen cookies*

## PEANUT BUTTER JUMBOS

- ½ cup butter, softened
- 1 cup packed brown sugar
- 1 cup granulated sugar
- 1½ cups peanut butter
- 3 eggs
- 2 teaspoons baking soda
- 1 teaspoon vanilla
- 4½ cups uncooked rolled oats
- 1 cup (6 ounces) semisweet chocolate chips
- 1 cup candy-coated chocolate pieces

Preheat oven to 350°F. Lightly grease cookie sheets or line with parchment paper.

Beat butter, sugars, peanut butter and eggs in large bowl until well blended. Blend in baking soda, vanilla and oats until well mixed. Stir in chocolate chips and candy pieces.

Scoop out about ⅓ cup dough for each cookie. Place on prepared cookie sheets, spacing about 4 inches apart. Press each cookie to flatten slightly. Bake 15 to 20 minutes or until firm in center. Remove to wire racks to cool.

*Makes about 1½ dozen cookies*

**Peanut Butter Jumbo Sandwiches:** Prepare cookies as directed. Place ⅓ cup softened chocolate or vanilla ice cream on cookie bottom. Top with cookie. Lightly press sandwich together. Repeat with remaining cookies. Wrap sandwiches in plastic wrap; freeze until firm.

## JAM–UP OATMEAL COOKIES

1 Butter Flavor* CRISCO® Stick or 1 cup
    Butter Flavor* CRISCO® all-vegetable
    shortening plus additional for
    greasing
1½ cups firmly packed brown sugar
  2 eggs
  2 teaspoons almond extract
  2 cups all-purpose flour
  1 teaspoon baking powder
  1 teaspoon salt
  ½ teaspoon baking soda
2½ cups quick oats (not instant or old
    fashioned), uncooked
  1 cup finely chopped pecans
  1 jar (12 ounces) strawberry jam
    Sugar for sprinkling

*Butter Flavor Crisco® is artificially flavored.*

**1.** Combine 1 cup shortening and brown sugar in large bowl. Beat at medium speed of electric mixer until well blended. Beat in eggs and almond extract.

**2.** Combine flour, baking powder, salt and baking soda. Mix into shortening mixture at low speed until just blended. Stir in oats and chopped nuts with spoon. Cover and refrigerate at least 1 hour.

**3.** Heat oven to 350°F. Grease baking sheets with shortening. Place sheets of foil on countertop for cooling cookies.

**4.** Roll out dough, half at a time, to about ¼-inch thickness on floured surface. Cut out with 2½-inch round cookie cutter. Place 1 teaspoonful of jam in center of half of the rounds. Top with remaining rounds. Press edges to seal. Prick centers; sprinkle with sugar. Place 1 inch apart on baking sheets.

**5.** Bake one baking sheet at a time at 350°F for 12 to 15 minutes or until lightly browned. *Do not overbake.* Cool 2 minutes on baking sheets. Remove cookies to foil to cool completely.

*Makes about 2 dozen cookies*

## DOUBLE CHOCOLATE OAT COOKIES

1 package (12 ounces) semi-sweet
    chocolate pieces, divided (about
    2 cups)
½ cup margarine or butter, softened
½ cup sugar
 1 egg
¼ teaspoon vanilla
¾ cup all-purpose flour
¾ cup QUAKER® Oats (quick or old
    fashioned, uncooked)
 1 teaspoon baking powder
¼ teaspoon baking soda
¼ teaspoon salt (optional)

Preheat oven to 375°F. Melt 1 cup chocolate pieces in small saucepan; set aside. Beat margarine and sugar until fluffy; add melted chocolate, egg and vanilla. Add combined flour, oats, baking powder, baking soda and salt; mix well. Stir in remaining chocolate pieces. Drop by rounded tablespoonfuls onto ungreased cookie sheet. Bake 8 to 10 minutes. Cool 1 minute on cookie sheet; remove to wire rack.

*Makes about 3 dozen cookies*

## BUTTER DROP–INS

### COOKIES
  ½ **Butter Flavor\* CRISCO® Stick or ½ cup
    Butter Flavor\* CRISCO® all-vegetable
    shortening plus additional for
    greasing**
  ¾ **cup granulated sugar**
  1 **tablespoon milk**
  1 **egg**
  ½ **teaspoon vanilla**
  1¼ **cups all-purpose flour**
  ¼ **teaspoon salt**
  ¼ **teaspoon baking powder**

### FROSTING
  ½ **Butter Flavor\* CRISCO® Stick or ½ cup
    Butter Flavor\* CRISCO® all-vegetable
    shortening**
  1 **pound (4 cups) confectioners' sugar**
  ⅓ **cup milk**
  1 **teaspoon vanilla**

*\*Butter Flavor Crisco® is artificially flavored.*

Heat oven to 375°F. Grease baking sheets.
Place sheets of foil on countertop for cooling
cookies. Combine ½ cup shortening,
granulated sugar and milk in medium bowl
at medium speed of electric mixer until well
blended. Beat in egg and vanilla. Combine
flour, salt and baking powder. Mix into
creamed mixture. Drop level measuring
tablespoonfuls 2 inches apart onto baking
sheet. Bake one baking sheet at a time at
375°F for 7 to 9 minutes. Remove cookies to
foil to cool completely.

For frosting, combine shortening,
confectioners' sugar, milk and vanilla in
small mixing bowl. Beat at low speed of
electric mixer for 15 seconds. Scrape bowl.
Beat at high speed for 2 minutes, or until
smooth and creamy. Frost cookies.

*Makes 1½ to 2 dozen cookies*

**Note:** Frosting can be tinted with food
coloring and piped decoratively onto cookies,
if desired.

**Prep Time:** 20 minutes
**Bake Time:** 7 to 9 minutes

## MINI PIZZA COOKIES

  1 **(20-ounce) tube of refrigerated sugar
    cookie dough**
  2 **cups (16 ounces) prepared pink frosting
    "M&M's"® Chocolate Mini Baking Bits
    Variety of additional toppings such as
    shredded coconut, granola, raisins,
    nuts, small pretzels, snack mixes,
    sunflower seeds, popped corn and
    mini marshmallows**

Preheat oven to 350°F. Lightly grease cookie
sheets; set aside. Divide dough into 8 equal
portions. On lightly floured surface, roll each
portion of dough into ¼-inch-thick circle;
place about 2 inches apart onto prepared
cookie sheets. Bake 10 to 13 minutes or until
golden brown on edges. Cool completely on
wire racks. Spread top of each pizza with
frosting; sprinkle with "M&M's"® Chocolate
Mini Baking Bits and 2 or 3 suggested
toppings.

*Makes 8 cookies*

*Mini Pizza Cookies*

## Buried Cherry Cookies

Chocolate Frosting (recipe follows)
½ cup butter or margarine, softened
1 cup sugar
1 egg
1½ teaspoons vanilla extract
1½ cups all-purpose flour
⅓ cup HERSHEY'S Cocoa
¼ teaspoon baking powder
¼ teaspoon baking soda
¼ teaspoon salt
1 jar (10 ounces) small maraschino cherries, drained

1. Prepare Chocolate Frosting; set aside. Heat oven to 350°F.

2. Beat butter, sugar, egg and vanilla in large bowl until light and fluffy. Stir together flour, cocoa, baking powder, baking soda and salt; gradually add to butter mixture, beating until well blended.

3. Shape dough into 1-inch balls. Place on ungreased cookie sheet about 2 inches apart. Press thumb in center of each ball to make indentation; place one cherry in each thumbprint.

4. Bake 10 minutes or until edges are set. Remove from cookie sheet to wire rack. Cool completely. Spoon scant teaspoonful frosting over each cherry, spreading to cover cherry.
*Makes about 3½ dozen cookies*

**Chocolate Frosting:** Place ⅔ cups sweetened condensed milk (not evaporated milk) and ½ cup HERSHEY'S Semi-Sweet Chocolate Chips in small microwave-safe bowl; stir. Microwave at HIGH (100%) 1 minute or until chips are melted and mixture is smooth when stirred. Cool completely. Makes 1 cup frosting.

## Giant Peanut Butter Cup Cookies

½ cup (1 stick) butter or margarine, softened
¾ cup sugar
⅓ cup REESE'S Creamy or Crunchy Peanut Butter
1 egg
½ teaspoon vanilla extract
1¼ cups all-purpose flour
½ teaspoon baking soda
¼ teaspoon salt
16 REESE'S Peanut Butter Cup Miniatures, cut into fourths

Heat oven to 350°F.

In small mixer bowl, beat butter, sugar and peanut butter until creamy. Add egg and vanilla; beat well. Stir together flour, baking soda and salt. Add to butter mixture; blend well. Drop dough by level ¼ cup measurements onto ungreased cookie sheets, three cookies per sheet. (Cookies will spread while baking.) Push about seven pieces of peanut butter cup into each cookie, flattening cookie slightly.

Bake 15 to 17 minutes or until light golden brown around the edges. Centers will be pale and slightly soft. Cool 1 minute on cookie sheet. Remove to wire rack; cool completely.
*Makes 9 cookies*

*Giant Peanut Butter Cup Cookies*

## BROWNIE TURTLE COOKIES

2 squares (1 ounce each) unsweetened
    baking chocolate
⅓ cup solid vegetable shortening
1 cup granulated sugar
½ teaspoon vanilla extract
2 large eggs
1¼ cups all-purpose flour
½ teaspoon baking powder
½ teaspoon salt
1 cup "M&M's"® Milk Chocolate Mini
    Baking Bits, divided
1 cup pecan halves
⅓ cup caramel ice cream topping
⅓ cup shredded coconut
⅓ cup finely chopped pecans

Preheat oven to 350°F. Lightly grease cookie
sheets; set aside. Heat chocolate and shortening
in 2-quart saucepan over low heat, stirring
constantly until melted; remove from heat.
Mix in sugar, vanilla and eggs. Blend in
flour, baking powder and salt. Stir in ⅔ *cup*
*"M&M's"® Milk Chocolate Mini Baking Bits.*
For each cookie, arrange 3 pecan halves, with
ends almost touching at center, on prepared
cookie sheets. Drop dough by rounded
teaspoonfuls onto center of each group of
pecans; mound the dough slightly. Bake
8 to 10 minutes just until set. *Do not overbake.*
Cool completely on wire racks. In small bowl
combine ice cream topping, coconut and nuts;
top each cookie with about 1½ teaspoons
mixture. Press remaining ⅓ *cup "M&M's"®*
*Milk Chocolate Mini Baking Bits* into
topping.     *Makes about 2½ dozen cookies*

## HAYSTACKS

¼ Butter Flavor* CRISCO® Stick or ¼ cup
    Butter Flavor* CRISCO® all-vegetable
    shortening
½ cup creamy peanut butter
2 cups butterscotch-flavored chips
6 cups corn flakes
⅔ cup semisweet miniature chocolate
    chips
    Chopped peanuts or chocolate jimmies
    (optional)

*\*Butter Flavor Crisco® is artificially flavored.*

**1.** Combine ¼ cup shortening, peanut butter
and butterscotch chips in large microwave-safe
bowl. Cover with waxed paper. Microwave at
50% (MEDIUM). Stir after 1 minute. Repeat
until smooth (or melt on rangetop in small
saucepan on very low heat, stirring
constantly).

**2.** Pour corn flakes into large bowl. Pour hot
butterscotch mixture over flakes. Stir with
spoon until flakes are coated. Stir in chocolate
chips.

**3.** Spoon ¼ cup of the mixture into mounds
on waxed paper-lined baking sheets. Sprinkle
with chopped nuts, if desired. Refrigerate
until firm.     *Makes about 3 dozen cookies*

*Brownie Turtle Cookies*

# BLISSFUL BARS

꧁꧂

## PHILLY® MARBLE BROWNIES

1 package (21½ ounces) brownie mix
1 package (8 ounces) PHILADELPHIA® Cream Cheese, softened
⅓ cup sugar
½ teaspoon vanilla
1 egg
1 cup BAKER'S® Semi-Sweet Real Chocolate Chips

PREPARE brownie mix as directed on package. Spread into greased 13×9-inch baking pan.

MIX cream cheese, sugar and vanilla with electric mixer on medium speed until well blended. Add egg; mix well. Pour over brownie mixture; cut through batter with knife several times for marble effect. Sprinkle with chips.

BAKE at 350°F for 35 to 40 minutes or until cream cheese mixture is lightly browned. Cool in pan on wire rack. Cut into squares.

*Makes 24 brownies*

Prep Time: 20 minutes plus cooling
Baking Time: 40 minutes

*PHILLY® Marble Brownies*

# BLISSFUL BARS

## TROPICAL COCONUT SQUARES

1 cup butter, softened
½ cup granulated sugar
2 egg yolks
¼ teaspoon salt
2¼ cups plus 3 tablespoons all-purpose
     flour, divided
½ teaspoon baking powder
1½ cups packed light brown sugar
3 eggs
1 teaspoon vanilla
1½ cups macadamia nuts
2 cups flaked coconut

Preheat oven to 350°F. Grease 15×10-inch
jelly-roll pan.

Beat butter and granulated sugar in large
bowl with electric mixer at medium speed
until light and fluffy. Beat in egg yolks and
salt. Gradually add 2¼ cups flour; beat at low
speed until well blended. Spread dough in
prepared pan. Bake 16 to 18 minutes or until
golden brown.

Meanwhile, combine remaining 3 tablespoons
flour and baking powder in small bowl. Beat
brown sugar and eggs in large bowl with
electric mixer at medium speed until very
thick. Beat in vanilla. Gradually add flour
mixture; beat at low speed until well blended.
Stir in nuts.

Spread batter evenly over hot crust; sprinkle
with coconut. Return pan to oven; bake 20 to
22 minutes or until topping is golden brown
and puffed. Remove pan to wire rack to cool
completely. Cut into 2-inch squares. Store
squares tightly covered at room temperature
or freeze up to 3 months.

*Makes about 40 squares*

## "CORDIALLY YOURS" CHOCOLATE CHIP BARS

¾ Butter Flavor* CRISCO® Stick or ¾ cup
     Butter Flavor* Crisco® all-vegetable
     shortening plus additional for
     greasing
2 eggs
½ cup granulated sugar
¼ cup firmly packed brown sugar
1½ teaspoons vanilla
1 teaspoon almond extract
2 cups all-purpose flour
1 teaspoon baking soda
½ teaspoon cinnamon
1 can (21 ounces) cherry pie filling
1½ cups milk chocolate chips
     Powdered sugar

*Butter Flavor Crisco® is artificially flavored.*

1. Preheat oven to 350°F. Grease 15½×10½×1-
inch pan.

2. Combine ¾ cup shortening, eggs,
granulated sugar, brown sugar, vanilla and
almond extract in large bowl. Beat at medium
speed of electric mixer until well blended.

3. Combine flour, baking soda and cinnamon.
Mix into creamed mixture at low speed until
just blended. Stir in pie filling and chocolate
chips. Spread in pan.

4. Bake 25 minutes or until lightly browned
and top springs back when lightly pressed.
Cool completely in pan on wire rack. Sprinkle
with powdered sugar. Cut into 2½×2-inch
bars.
*Makes 30 bars*

## RICH AND FUDGY FROSTED BROWNIES

8 ounces unsweetened chocolate
1 cup butter
3 cups sugar
5 eggs
2 tablespoons light corn syrup
1 tablespoon vanilla extract
1¾ cups all-purpose flour
1 cup coarsely chopped nuts (optional)
   Frosting (recipe follows)

Preheat oven to 375°F. Melt chocolate and butter in medium saucepan over low heat, stirring constantly. Set aside and let cool. Beat sugar, eggs, corn syrup and vanilla in large bowl with electric mixer on high speed 10 minutes. Blend in chocolate mixture on low speed. Add flour, beating just until blended. Stir in nuts, if desired. Spread in greased 13×9-inch pan. Bake 30 to 35 minutes. *Do not overbake.* Cool completely before frosting.

*Makes 24 brownies*

### FROSTING

6 tablespoons butter or margarine, softened
⅓ cup unsweetened cocoa powder
2⅔ cups powdered sugar
⅓ cup milk
1 tablespoon vanilla extract

Beat butter in small bowl until creamy. Add cocoa and powdered sugar alternately with milk; beat until frosting is of spreading consistency. Stir in vanilla. Spread on cooled brownies.

*Favorite recipe from* **Bob Evans**®

## CHEWY RED RASPBERRY BARS

1 cup firmly packed light brown sugar
½ cup butter or margarine, room temperature
½ teaspoon almond extract
1 cup all-purpose flour
1 cup quick-cooking or old-fashioned oats
1 teaspoon baking powder
½ cup SMUCKER'S® Red Raspberry Preserves

Combine brown sugar and butter; beat until fluffy. Beat in almond extract. Mix in flour, oats and baking powder until crumbly. Reserve ¼ cup mixture; pat remaining mixture into bottom of greased 8-inch square baking pan. Dot preserves over crumb mixture in pan; sprinkle with reserved crumb mixture.

Bake at 350°F for 30 to 40 minutes or until brown. Cool on wire rack. Cut into bars.

*Makes 12 bars*

*Replacing the butter or margarine in a recipe with a spread, diet margarine, whipped butter or whipped margarine may result in an inferior cookie or brownie. For best results, use the product called for in the recipe.*

## DOUBLE CHOCOLATE CRISPY BARS

6 cups crispy rice cereal
½ cup peanut butter
⅓ cup butter
2 squares (1 ounce each) unsweetened
   chocolate
1 package (8 ounces) marshmallows
1 cup (6 ounces) semisweet chocolate
   chips *or* 6 ounces bittersweet
   chocolate, chopped
6 ounces white chocolate, chopped
2 teaspoons shortening, divided

Preheat oven to 350°F. Line 13×9-inch pan
with waxed paper. Spread cereal on cookie
sheet; toast in oven 10 minutes or until crispy;
place in large bowl. Meanwhile, combine
peanut butter, butter and unsweetened
chocolate in large heavy saucepan. Stir over
low heat until chocolate is melted. Add
marshmallows; stir until melted and smooth.
Pour chocolate mixture over cereal; mix until
evenly coated. Press firmly into prepared pan.
Place semisweet and white chocolates into
separate bowls. Add 1 teaspoon shortening
to each bowl. Place bowls over very warm
water; stir until chocolates are melted. Spread
top of bars with melted semisweet chocolate;
cool until chocolate is set. Turn bars out of
pan onto waxed paper, chocolate side down.
Remove waxed paper from bottom of bars;
spread white chocolate over surface. Cool
until chocolate is set. Cut into 2×1½-inch bars.
*Makes about 3 dozen bars*

## MARBLED PEANUT BUTTER BROWNIES

⅔ cup all-purpose or whole wheat flour
½ teaspoon baking powder
¼ teaspoon salt
¾ cup firmly packed brown sugar
½ cup SMUCKER'S® Creamy Natural
   Peanut Butter or LAURA
   SCUDDER'S® Smooth Old-Fashioned
   Peanut Butter
¼ cup butter or margarine, softened
2 eggs
1 teaspoon vanilla
3 (1-ounce) squares semisweet chocolate
   or ½ cup semisweet chocolate chips,
   melted and cooled

Combine flour, baking powder and salt; set
aside.

In small bowl of electric mixer, combine
brown sugar, peanut butter and butter; beat
until light and creamy. Add eggs and vanilla;
beat until fluffy. Stir in flour mixture just until
blended. Spread in greased 8-inch square
baking pan. Drizzle chocolate over batter, then
swirl into batter with table knife to marbleize.

Bake in preheated 350°F oven 25 to 30 minutes
or until toothpick inserted in center comes
out clean. Cool in pan on rack. Cut into bars.
*Makes 24 bars*

## GOOEY CARAMEL CHOCOLATE BARS

2 cups all-purpose flour
1 cup granulated sugar
¼ teaspoon salt
2 cups (4 sticks) butter, divided
1 cup packed light brown sugar
⅓ cup light corn syrup
1 cup (6 ounces) semisweet chocolate chips

Preheat oven to 350°F. Line 13×9-inch baking pan with foil. Combine flour, granulated sugar and salt in medium bowl; stir until blended. Cut in 14 tablespoons (1¾ sticks) butter until mixture resembles coarse crumbs. Press onto bottom of prepared pan.

Bake 18 to 20 minutes or until lightly browned around edges. Remove pan to wire rack; cool completely.

Combine 1 cup (2 sticks) butter, brown sugar and corn syrup in heavy medium saucepan. Cook over medium heat 5 to 8 minutes or until mixture boils, stirring frequently. Boil gently 2 minutes, without stirring. Immediately pour over cooled base; spread evenly to edges of pan with metal spatula. Cool completely.

Melt chocolate in double boiler over hot (not boiling) water. Stir in remaining 2 tablespoons butter. Pour over cooled caramel layer and spread evenly to edges of pan with metal spatula. Refrigerate 10 to 15 minutes until chocolate begins to set. Remove; cool completely. Cut into bars.

*Makes 3 dozen bars*

## RASPBERRY WALNUT BARS

1¾ cups all-purpose flour, divided
¾ cup margarine or butter, softened
1⅓ cups packed light brown sugar, divided
½ cup raspberry preserves
½ cup egg substitute
1 teaspoon salt
1 teaspoon DAVIS® Baking Powder
½ cup PLANTERS® Walnuts, chopped
    Powdered Sugar Glaze (recipe follows, optional)

**1.** Mix 1½ cups flour, margarine and ⅓ cup brown sugar in large bowl with mixer at low speed; press mixture onto bottom of ungreased 13×9×2-inch baking pan.

**2.** Bake in preheated 350°F oven for 18 to 20 minutes. Spread raspberry preserves over baked layer.

**3.** Mix remaining flour, brown sugar, egg substitute, salt and baking powder in medium bowl. Spread over raspberry layer; sprinkle with walnuts.

**4.** Bake at 350°F for 18 to 20 minutes or until done. Cool on wire rack. Drizzle with Powdered Sugar Glaze, if desired. Cut into bars. *Makes 2 dozen bars*

**Powdered Sugar Glaze:** Combine 1 cup powdered sugar and 5 to 6 teaspoons water.

**Preparation Time:** 20 minutes
**Cook Time:** 36 minutes
**Total Time:** 56 minutes

## MISSISSIPPI MUD BARS

¾ cup packed brown sugar
½ cup butter, softened
1 egg
1 teaspoon vanilla
½ teaspoon baking soda
¼ teaspoon salt
1 cup plus 2 tablespoons all-purpose flour
1 cup (6 ounces) semisweet chocolate
   chips, divided
1 cup (6 ounces) white chocolate chips,
   divided
½ cup chopped walnuts or pecans

Preheat oven to 375°F. Line a 9-inch square pan with foil; grease foil. Beat sugar and butter in large bowl until blended and smooth. Beat in egg and vanilla until light. Blend in baking soda and salt. Add flour, mixing until well blended. Stir in ¾ cup each semisweet and white chocolate chips and nuts. Spread dough in prepared pan. Bake 23 to 25 minutes or until center feels firm. *Do not overbake.* Remove from oven; sprinkle remaining ¼ cup each semisweet and white chocolate chips over top. Let stand until chips melt; spread evenly over bars. Cool in pan on wire rack until chocolate is set. Cut into 2×1-inch bars.

*Makes about 3 dozen bars*

*Gooey Caramel Chocolate Bars*

## CINNAMONY APPLE STREUSEL BARS

1¼ cups all-purpose flour
1¼ cups graham cracker crumbs
¾ cup packed brown sugar, divided
¼ cup granulated sugar
1 teaspoon ground cinnamon
¾ cup butter, melted
2 cups chopped peeled apples (2 medium)
Glaze (recipe follows)

Preheat oven to 350°F. Grease 13×9-inch baking pan. Combine flour, graham cracker crumbs, ½ cup brown sugar, granulated sugar, cinnamon and melted butter in large bowl until well blended; reserve 1 cup. Press remaining crumb mixture into bottom of prepared pan.

Bake 8 minutes. Remove from oven; set aside. Toss apples with remaining ¼ cup brown sugar in medium bowl until brown sugar is dissolved; arrange apples over baked crust. Sprinkle reserved 1 cup crumb mixture over filling. Bake 30 to 35 minutes more or until apples are tender. Remove pan to wire rack; cool completely. Drizzle with Glaze. Cut into bars. *Makes 3 dozen bars*

**Glaze:** Combine ½ cup powdered sugar and 1 tablespoon milk in small bowl until well blended.

## O'HENRIETTA BARS

MAZOLA® NO STICK® Cooking Spray
½ cup (1 stick) MAZOLA® Margarine or butter, softened
½ cup packed brown sugar
½ cup KARO® Light or Dark Corn Syrup
1 teaspoon vanilla
3 cups quick oats, uncooked
½ cup (3 ounces) semisweet chocolate chips
¼ cup SKIPPY® Creamy Peanut Butter

**1.** Preheat oven to 350°F. Spray 8- or 9-inch square baking pan with cooking spray.

**2.** In large bowl with mixer at medium speed, beat margarine, brown sugar, corn syrup and vanilla until smooth. Stir in oats. Press into prepared pan.

**3.** Bake 25 minutes or until center is barely firm. Cool on wire rack 5 minutes.

**4.** Sprinkle with chocolate chips; top with small spoonfuls of peanut butter. Let stand 5 minutes; spread peanut butter and chocolate over bars, swirling to marbleize.

**5.** Cool completely on wire rack before cutting. Cut into bars; refrigerate 15 minutes to set topping. *Makes 24 bars*

**Prep Time:** 20 minutes
**Bake Time:** 25 minutes, plus cooling

*Cinnamony Apple Streusel Bars*

## BUTTERY LEMON BARS

**CRUST**
- 1¼ cups all-purpose flour
- ½ cup butter, softened
- ¼ cup powdered sugar
- ½ teaspoon vanilla

**FILLING**
- 1 cup granulated sugar
- 2 eggs
- ⅓ cup fresh lemon juice
- 2 tablespoons all-purpose flour
- Grated peel of 1 lemon
- Powdered sugar

**1.** Preheat oven to 350°F.

**2.** Combine all crust ingredients in small bowl. Beat at low speed 2 to 3 minutes until mixture is crumbly. Press onto bottom of 8-inch square baking pan. Bake 15 to 20 minutes or until edges are lightly browned.

**3.** Combine all filling ingredients except powdered sugar in small bowl. Beat at low speed until well mixed.

**4.** Pour filling over hot crust. Continue baking 15 to 18 minutes or until filling is set. Sprinkle with powdered sugar; cool completely. Cut into bars; sprinkle again with powdered sugar. *Makes about 16 bars*

## HERSHEY'S PREMIUM DOUBLE CHOCOLATE BROWNIES

- ¾ cup HERSHEY®S Cocoa
- ½ teaspoon baking soda
- ⅔ cup butter or margarine, melted and divided
- ½ cup boiling water
- 2 cups sugar
- 2 eggs
- 1 teaspoon vanilla extract
- 1⅓ cups all-purpose flour
- ¼ teaspoon salt
- 2 cups (12-ounce package) HERSHEY®S Semi-Sweet Chocolate Chips
- ½ cup coarsely chopped nuts (optional)

**1.** Heat oven to 350°F. Grease 13×9×2-inch baking pan.

**2.** Stir together cocoa and baking soda in large bowl; stir in ⅓ cup butter. Add boiling water; stir until mixture thickens. Stir in sugar, eggs, remaining ⅓ cup butter and vanilla; stir until smooth. Gradually add flour and salt to cocoa mixture, beating until well blended. Stir in chocolate chips and nuts, if desired; pour batter into prepared pan.

**3.** Bake 35 to 40 minutes or until brownies begin to pull away from sides of pan. Cool completely in pan on wire rack. Cut into bars. *Makes about 36 brownies*

## CRISPY CHOCOLATE BARS

1 package (6 ounces, 1 cup) semi-sweet
   chocolate chips
1 package (6 ounces, 1 cup) butterscotch
   chips
½ cup peanut butter
5 cups KELLOGG'S CORN FLAKES®
   cereal
   Vegetable cooking spray

**1.** In large saucepan, combine chocolate and butterscotch chips and peanut butter. Stir over low heat until smooth. Remove from heat.

**2.** Add Kellogg's Corn Flakes® cereal. Stir until well coated.

**3.** Using buttered spatula or waxed paper, press mixture evenly into 9×9×2-inch pan coated with cooking spray. Cut into bars when cool. *Makes 16 bars*

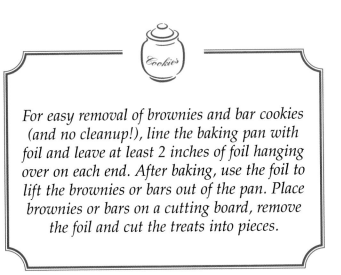

*For easy removal of brownies and bar cookies (and no cleanup!), line the baking pan with foil and leave at least 2 inches of foil hanging over on each end. After baking, use the foil to lift the brownies or bars out of the pan. Place brownies or bars on a cutting board, remove the foil and cut the treats into pieces.*

## DOUBLE CHOCOLATE BARS

1½ cups all-purpose flour
 ¼ cup unsweetened cocoa
 1 teaspoon baking soda
 ½ cup FLEISCHMANN'S® Original
   Margarine, softened
 ¾ cup packed dark brown sugar
 ½ cup granulated sugar
 ¼ cup EGG BEATERS® Healthy Real Egg
   Substitute
 1 teaspoon vanilla extract
 1 cup reduced-fat chocolate-flavored
   baking chips

**1.** Mix flour, cocoa and baking soda in small bowl; set aside.

**2.** Blend margarine, sugars, egg substitute and vanilla in large bowl with mixer at medium speed until smooth. Stir in flour mixture until blended; stir in chips. Press dough in greased 13×9×2-inch baking pan.

**3.** Bake in preheated 350°F oven for 18 minutes or until done. Cool completely on wire rack; cut into bars. *Makes 32 bars*

**Preparation Time:** 15 minutes
**Cook Time:** 18 minutes
**Total Time:** 33 minutes

## PECAN PIE BARS

¾ cup butter, softened
½ cup powdered sugar
1½ cups all-purpose flour
3 eggs
2 cups coarsely chopped pecans
1 cup granulated sugar
1 cup light corn syrup
2 tablespoons butter, melted
1 teaspoon vanilla

Preheat oven to 350°F. For crust, beat butter in large bowl with electric mixer at medium speed until smooth. Add powdered sugar; beat at medium speed until well blended.

Add flour gradually, beating at low speed after each addition. (Mixture will be crumbly but presses together easily.)

Press dough evenly into ungreased 13×9-inch baking pan. Press mixture slightly up sides of pan (less than ¼ inch) to form lip to hold filling.

Bake 20 to 25 minutes or until golden brown. Meanwhile, for filling, beat eggs lightly in medium bowl with fork. Add pecans, granulated sugar, corn syrup, melted butter and vanilla; mix well.

Pour filling over partially baked crust. Return to oven; bake 35 to 40 minutes or until filling is set.

Loosen edges with knife. Let cool completely on wire rack before cutting into squares. Cover and refrigerate until 10 to 15 minutes before serving time. (Do not freeze.)

*Makes about 48 bars*

## SPICED DATE BARS

½ cup margarine, softened
1 cup packed brown sugar
2 eggs
¾ cup light sour cream
2 cups all-purpose flour
1 teaspoon baking soda
1 teaspoon ground cinnamon
½ teaspoon ground nutmeg
1 package (8 or 10 ounces) DOLE®
    Chopped Dates or Pitted Dates,
    chopped
Powdered sugar (optional)

• Beat margarine and brown sugar until light and fluffy. Beat in eggs, one at a time. Stir in sour cream.

• Combine dry ingredients. Beat into sour cream, stir in dates. Spread batter evenly into greased 13×9-inch baking pan.

• Bake at 350°F 25 to 30 minutes or until toothpick inserted in center comes out clean. Cool completely in pan on wire rack. Cut into bars. Dust with powdered sugar.

*Makes 24 bars*

**Prep Time:** 15 minutes
**Bake Time:** 30 minutes

*Pecan Pie Bars*

## CHOCOLATE CHIP BROWNIES

¾ cup granulated sugar
½ cup butter
2 tablespoons water
2 cups semisweet chocolate chips or mini chocolate chips, divided
1½ teaspoons vanilla
1¼ cups all-purpose flour
½ teaspoon baking soda
½ teaspoon salt
2 eggs
Powdered sugar (optional)

Preheat oven to 350°F. Grease 9-inch square baking pan.

Combine sugar, butter and water in medium microwavable mixing bowl. Microwave on HIGH 2½ to 3 minutes or until butter is melted. Stir in 1 cup chocolate chips; stir gently until chips are melted and mixture is well blended. Stir in vanilla; let stand 5 minutes to cool.

Combine flour, baking soda and salt in small bowl. Beat eggs into chocolate mixture, 1 at a time. Add flour mixture; mix well. Stir in remaining 1 cup chocolate chips. Spread batter evenly into prepared pan.

Bake 25 minutes for fudgy brownies or 30 to 35 minutes for cakelike brownies. Remove pan to wire rack to cool completely. Cut into 2¼-inch squares. Place powdered sugar in fine-mesh strainer and sprinkle over brownies, if desired. Store tightly covered at room temperature or freeze up to 3 months.

*Makes 16 brownies*

*Chocolate Chip Brownies*

#  ACKNOWLEDGMENTS

**The publishers would like to thank the companies listed below for the use of their recipes in this publication.**

Bestfoods

Blue Diamond Growers®

Bob Evans®

Dole Food Company, Inc.

Duncan Hines® brand is a registered trademark of Aurora Foods Inc.

Egg Beaters® Healthy Real Egg Substitute

Fleischmann's® Original Spread

Hershey Foods Corporation

Kellogg Company

Kraft Foods, Inc.

M&M/MARS

PLANTERS® Baking Nuts

The Procter & Gamble Company

The Quaker® Kitchens

The J.M. Smucker Company

Sunkist Growers

Wisconsin Milk Marketing Board

# INDEX